MUSTARD

Edible

Series Editor: Andrew F. Smith

EDIBLE is a revolutionary series of books dedicated to food and drink that explores the rich history of cuisine. Each book reveals the global history and culture of one type of food or beverage.

Already published

Mustard

A Global History

Demet Güzey

REAKTION BOOKS

To Luca and Adriano – team boys

Published by Reaktion Books Ltd
Unit 32, Waterside
44–48 Wharf Road
London N1 7UX, UK
www.reaktionbooks.co.uk

First published 2019

Printed and bound in China by 1010 Printing International Ltd

A catalogue record for this book is available from the British Library

ISBN 978 1 78914 143 6

Contents

Introduction

A seed contains life. It creates a plant, flowers and new seeds. Its cyclical nature is mundane and magnificent at the same time. So is the mustard seed. In its simplicity there is potency, permanence and timelessness.

Mustard is among the top three most used condiments in the world, sharing the stage with salt and pepper. It has been in the pantry of history for at least 4,000 years, and in written recipes in Europe since the second century. Mustard is more than a condiment; it is the embodiment of civilization, because the story of mustard is a story of medicine, myth and magic. Mustard is stimulating and potent but also simple and down-to-earth; it gives a lot of taste to a variety of dishes without the unhealthy connotations some condiments have. It has been the spice of the poor and the condiment of the rich. Its history is full of inventions, royal awards and medals. In this, mustard is an item of personal choice as well as national pride.

From mayonnaise to sauces, hot dogs to pretzels, soups to salads and meats, mustard accompanies and flavours our food around the world. This global life of mustard can be traced in cookbooks and advertisements, popular culture, literature and religious texts. This book aims to illustrate the importance of mustard in culinary history. The opening chapter defines mustard as a plant, seed and a condiment. Chapter Two looks at types of mustard around the world, whether grainy or smooth; spicy or sweet; Dijon, American or English; or made into powder, sauces or balls. Chapter Three is dedicated to the symbolism that has been given to mustard in religion, literature and idioms, and explains how mustard came to be a symbol of strength, small beginnings, growth, faith and enthusiasm. Chapter Four tells the medical use of mustard as a treatment for illnesses, such as digestion and the common cold, for which it has been chewed as seeds, used as plasters or combined with other foods to balance their properties. Last but not least we explore the use of mustard sauce and oil in the kitchen, as an indispensable ingredient to many traditional dishes. The applications of mustard are as many as its seeds. The recipe section focuses mainly on historical and new ways to make mustard condiment and sauces, as well as their use in some of the iconic mustard dishes around the world.

Please pass the mustard!

I
The Meaning of Mustard

The mustard plant belongs to the family Brassicaceae, otherwise known as the Cruciferae, as its flower petals resemble a cross. Other members of the family include cole vegetables such as radishes, turnips, cress and horseradish, and weeds such as wild mustard or charlock.

Mustard is a plant, a seed and a powder; it yields an oil, a condiment and an ingredient. It is used in food, in rituals, as forage for sheep, as green manure and even as biofuel for an intercontinental Boeing 787 Dreamliner.[1] Some runners today eat packets of mustard while racing in order to prevent cramps. Mustard has been used as medicine and for seasoning food since prehistoric times. It has been found in the tombs of Egyptian pharaohs and in the caves of Europe and China. Its seeds grow easily in a variety of climates, require minimal processing and have always been available to all levels in society.

The name 'mustard' was born when the Romans mixed unfermented grape juice, must (Latin *mustum*), with ground mustard seeds and made a hot must, *mustum ardens*. Most countries in Europe have similar names for the condiment: it is called mustard in English, *moutarde* in French, *mostaza* in Spanish and *mosterd* in Dutch; in Hindi it is *sarson*, and in Arabic

Black mustard from a drawing in *Medizinal Pflanzen* by Franz Eugen Köhler.

khardal, both suggesting a unique origin, independent of the Roman influence.

Mustard seeds come in three species identified by their colours: yellow, brown and black. Yellow or white mustard (*Sinapis alba*, also called *Brassica hirta*) is best known as the main ingredient in the mustard that flavours North America's traditional hot dog. Brown mustard, *Brassica juncea*, has a dark brown seed coat and is used in the manufacturing of Dijon-style mustards. Brown mustard is used in combination with yellow in the making of English-style mustard. What we call oriental mustard is the golden yellow seed coat version of *Brassica juncea*. The main market for oriental mustard is South and East Asia, where it is used as a condiment in Japanese cuisine and as a source of cooking oil in some other countries, especially India and Nepal. The Chinese spicy mustard *gai* and the Japanese mustard *karashi*, both made from brown mustard seeds, are used in soy dipping sauces. The leaves of various varieties of *Brassica juncea* are also the source of mustard greens. Black mustard (*Brassica nigra*) is native to tropical regions of North Africa, temperate regions of Europe and parts of Asia. It is the type that is commonly used in Indian cuisine and Chinese medicine and the one that is mentioned in the Bible and in many historical recipes.

Horseradish (*Armoracia rusticana*) and its Japanese cousin wasabi (*Wasabia japonica*) are closely related to mustard. For

Yellow, oriental and brown mustard seeds.

wasabi the stem of the plant is grated, dried into a powder or made into a paste; for horseradish the roots are grated and often mixed with vinegar. These three are the most pungent members of the Brassicaceae family.

Mustard seeds are approximately 1–2 millimetres (0.04– 0.08 in.) in diameter with a spherical shape. Because they are so tiny, a small quantity plants a large area. The plant reaches a height of about 1 to 1.5 metres (3–5 ft) and produces small bright-yellow flowers in the spring. As the mustard flower grows and matures, it forms pods with seeds inside. In the late summer, usually early August, the pods begin to ripen. Mustard pods are harvested when the plant dries out. The crop is cut and fed into combines where the pods are crushed open and the seeds are collected.

The top three producers of mustard seeds in the world are Canada, Nepal and Myanmar, together accounting for about 70 per cent of the world's mustard seed crop. Production in Canada, the United States and by European countries is mainly for the condiment and spice trade. In Asia, instead, the seeds are worked into mustard cooking oil, as the average oil content of a seed is 40 per cent by weight. However, the biggest users of the seed are not its top producers. The United States is the most important destination for mustard seed and Germany is the second largest importer.[2]

The leaves of the mustard plant are eaten as mustard greens, and the seeds are used as a spice, pressed to make mustard oil, or ground and mixed with water and vinegar to obtain the yellow condiment we call mustard. The word 'condiment' comes from the Latin verb *condire*, which means 'to season'.

Culinary uses of mustard were well-recorded in the ancient world. Athenaeus' third-century CE *Deipnosophists* mentioned mixing vinegar and grape must with pounded raisins and mustard seeds for a turnip dish. The combination of sweet and bitter or pungent flavours was common in Roman recipes, too. Several condiments such as coriander, celery and mustard would be mixed with wine, vinegar, must, fruit juice, fish sauce, oil, milk and/or honey to make sauces for birds and other meat.[3]

One of the first mustard recipes in the Western world appeared in the Roman cookbook *De re coquinaria* (On the Subject of Cooking), from the late fourth or early fifth century, as a sauce for various meats. Some such recipes called

Signboard for the mustard company Amora, painted carved oak. It was used at the Dijon Gastronomy Fair in 1930.

for a whole pantry list of ingredients next to ground mustard: pepper, caraway, lovage, grilled coriander seeds, dill, celery, thyme, oregano, onion, honey, vinegar, fish sauce and oil.

In the Middle Ages, mustard was the condiment of the poor. Imported spices were expensive and therefore out of reach for most of society, so instead common, locally grown seasonings were popular: onions, garlic, parsley, thyme and mustard.[4] Medieval spices, including mustard, were used not only to flavour foods but to balance them. Spices balanced the food with bodily humours, according to the dietetic rules advanced by the ancient Greek physician Hippocrates and developed by Greek physicians of antiquity, particularly Galen. Humorism was a system of medicine, which explained the body in four fluids, directly linked to temperament and health. These four humours were black bile, yellow bile, phlegm and blood. According to this theory, our body is filled with these substances and they have to be in balance for us to be healthy. These four humours are related to the four elements: earth, fire, water and air. They are also related to the four seasons, four ages of life, and specific organs. In treating humours, food was thought to have a direct effect on remedying any imbalances. The humour of any food was defined as a mixture of two qualities: temperature and moisture. Warm and moist substances tended towards the sanguine, cold and moist towards the phlegmatic, cold and dry to the melancholic and warm and dry to the bilious. Spices with a hot and dry character, such as pepper, cinnamon and mustard, could be used to make cold and moist dishes, like meats, more digestible. Mustard was hot and dry of the fourth (highest) degree and this degree of hotness could be dangerous if it were consumed alone. The master physician Aldobrandino of Siena in his *Regimen sanitatis* (Rule of Health, 1500) wrote of mustard: 'You should know that its heat decreases if it is distempered with vinegar; and if it is distempered with new wine, it is not quite so dry.' Verjuice and vinegar were both cool liquids that would 'distemper' the effect of mustard.[5]

In the fourteenth century, Magninus (Maino de Maineri), a Milanese physician, devoted an entire book, *Opusculum de saporibus* (Little Work on Flavours, 1364), to sauces. He permitted flavour to be the guiding principle over dietetics and declared that delicious sauces encouraged digestion and health. Magninus proposed a mustard sauce for boiled pork which contained rocket (arugula), mustard, sweet spices, verjuice and pork fat pounded in a mortar with white onions, buttery cheese and beef marrow. It could also be made with almond milk and pomegranate wine or verjuice, sweet spices and eggs thickened with verjuice.[6]

Being a professional cook in the late Middle Ages meant knowing how to prepare appetizing dishes that would above all ensure the good health of one's employer. A cook therefore had to know all of the 'evil' qualities of the foodstuffs and how to compensate for them. For example, the fifteenth-century Renaissance writer and gastronomist Bartolomeo Sacchi, known as Platina, wrote: 'The bean is hot and moist but its noxiousness can be tempered with a sprinkle of oregano, pepper and mustard, and an accompaniment of dry wine.'

By the sixteenth century, there was a conflict between cooking and medicine. The French dietitian Charles Estienne, one of the adversaries of mustard, condemned sauces with mustard seeds, vinegar and pickles. He called salt, verjuice and vinegar vulgar condiments and considered many sauces, and especially mustard, harmful for the stomach.[7]

In the late Renaissance, sauces no longer followed dietetic standards of contrasting and correcting meats, but rather of reinforcing their qualities. Sauces based on butter and meat juices became more popular, following the court

Enamel on copper mustard pot, British, South Staffordshire, *c.* 1770.

American Parian porcelain mustard pot, 1830–70, and a silver mustard spoon from 18th-century Germany.

fashion. By the eighteenth century in Europe attention to dietetic principles of absorption and the medicinal qualities of food had faded away.

For centuries, no table in Europe was complete without mustard, whether it came in a glass, earthenware, silver or tin pot. In Dijon the mustard pots were tall, glazed earthenware with a narrow neck and a curved rim to prevent exposure to oxygen, which causes darkening of colour and loss of flavour. First they were inscribed by hand with the maker's name and later they were decorated with a print roller and a stencil. Fine ceramic mustard pots were made in Faenza, Italy, in the fourteenth century. In sixteenth-century Delft, in the Netherlands, blue-and-white tin-glazed earthenware mustard pots were decorated in an oriental style. After the seventeenth century metal pots with pedestal bases and domed lids were in fashion. Their lids had an opening that held a spoon, some of which were very finely decorated.

Nowadays, basic mustard is made from ground, whole or cracked mustard seeds (yellow, brown or black), water, vinegar, and flavourings and spices, such as turmeric and paprika. For yellow mustard, the powdered ingredients of salts and spices (5 per cent of content) are mixed with water (60 per cent) and vinegar (20 per cent), and mustard seeds (15 per cent) go in last. Ingredients are blended at high speed before being transferred to a stone mill, which grinds the mixture into a thick and creamy bright yellow mustard. This heats the mustard to 60 degrees Celsius (140°F). A finesse test (also called a slick test) is done by spreading some mustard on a metal bar with grooves to confirm that the particle size is small enough before bottling. The mustard is deaerated, cooled overnight and bottled the day after. For Dijon and English mustard the process is slightly different, as we will see later.

The Chemistry Behind the Pungency of Mustard

Mustard seed is not spicy until it is crushed. Mustard and its relatives have two kinds of defensive chemicals in their tissue, which release the typical flavours of mustard when they are in contact: flavour precursors (called glucosinolates) and enzymes (myrosinase) that act on the precursors to free the flavours. When the plant cells are damaged or the seed is crushed these two are mixed and generate bitter, pungent and smelly compounds, as in cabbage, broccoli and onion.

The addition of hot water or vinegar inactivates the enzyme myrosinase, making the mustard milder.

Growing temperatures affect the amount of flavour precursors. Higher temperatures and drought increase their quantity while milder temperatures and humidity decrease them. Therefore, the mustards harvested in hot and dry climates have a stronger and more pungent taste. Mustard seeds, especially black mustard and, to a lesser extent, yellow mustard, contain sinigrin, a glucosinolate that belongs to the family of glucosides. Whenever sinigrin-containing plant tissue is crushed or otherwise damaged, the enzyme myrosinase degrades sinigrin to a mustard oil (allyl isothiocyanate), which is responsible for the pungent taste of mustard. Seeds of white mustard give much less pungent mustard because this species contains a different glucosinolate, sinalbin.

The food science writer Harold McGee defines mustard's pungency as 'neither a taste nor a smell, but a general feeling of irritation that verges on pain'.[8] We perceive pungency in mustard (and in its relatives horseradish and wasabi) because thiocyanates, small molecules that are released from the food into the air and up into our nasal passages, stimulate our nerve endings, which then send a message of pain to the brain. Some treatments, such as soaking and chopping, increase the release of these molecules and therefore pungency and pain, and some others, like fermentation and heating, decrease them.

We can thank caterpillars for the pungency of our mustards. The mustard plant defends itself against insects by producing glucosinolates. Some insects, however, such as the caterpillars of cabbage butterflies, evolved resistance to these glucosinates over millions of years. Since they could still eat the plant, the plant produced much more of the glucosinates to protect against the caterpillars. The caterpillars adapted and the plant produced even more glucosinates, and so on. This competition to gain advantage over each other diversified the mustard plant and the butterfly species. More than 120 different types of glucosinolates are produced by plants today.

When talking about the pungency of mustard, another substance comes to mind: mustard gas. However, it has no link whatsoever to the mustard plant. Mustard gas was a sulphur-based product, synthesized for the First World War. It received its name simply because it smelled like mustard.

2
The Mustard Manual

The oldest mustard seeds known are the carbonized seeds from 4800 BCE found in archaeological vessels in western China. This was the pungent black mustard, which is not widely cultivated today. Brown mustard originated in northwest India and white/yellow mustard in the Mediterranean. However, black mustard found at military, rural and settlement sites of the Roman imperial period in northwest Europe suggest that it was likely produced locally on a small scale there, too.[1]

The ancient Greeks and Romans transformed mustard seeds into a smooth and aromatic medicinal paste. After mustard proved its use in medicine, it quickly moved to the kitchen. The Romans would combine the seeds with unfermented grape juice to create what they called 'burning juice', *mustum ardens*. They imported the use of table mustard to Gaul and Burgundy, although mustard was most likely growing freely all over the Mediterranean. Mustard cultivation picked up in France by the ninth century. From there it spread to Germany, then to England and Spain. The Spanish have been credited for introducing it to the Americas during the colonization of Upper (Alta) California in the eighteenth century.

Gold mustard with white truffle flavour and olive oil.

In the Middle Ages, mustard grew like a weed in Europe. It was used by the poor to replace pepper, which at that time was a very expensive imported spice. During the Renaissance, mustard found its way onto the tables of the more privileged classes as a ready-to-serve sauce prepared by famed vinegar makers. As the production of mustard sauce became

Mustard seeds, flour and sauces.

more industrialized in the eighteenth and early nineteenth centuries, it became increasingly available to the masses as a condiment.

Across the centuries some countries became known for making mustard, and each such country developed their characteristics for colour, spiciness and texture, from smooth to wholegrain mustard to mustard powder. The variety of mustards include Dijon mustard, English mustard, American yellow mustard, Bavarian sweet mustard, Japanese *karashi* mustard, Bengali *kasundi* and the fruit mustards, *mostarda*, of Italy.

French Mustard

Mustard is the king of condiments in France. Since the Middle Ages, mustard has been made in Paris and in various wine-producing areas of the country such as Bordeaux and Burgundy. However, French mustard is not limited to one type. It ranges from the grainy *moutarde à l'ancienne* to the coarsely crushed mustard of Meaux, from the dark-coloured mustard of Bordeaux to the claret-coloured mild mustard of Beaujolais and the purplish Violette mustard from Brive. And there are many others that are flavoured by fruits, herbs and spices.

Mustard came to France when the Romans colonized Gaul (now France) and brought grape vines, aqueducts, roads and recipes. Charlemagne – the king of the Franks and later the ruler of the Holy Roman Empire, also considered to be the father of Europe after uniting most of the continent in his reign in the early 800s – ordered the cultivation of mustard in the botanical gardens around monasteries in France. Hence the production of mustard in France started around this time. Within a few centuries France and especially Dijon, the capital of Burgundy, became famous for its mustard.

The words *moutarde* and *sénevé* were introduced into the French language in the thirteenth century. Mustard makers and merchants were called *moutardiers*. *Moutardier* as an occupation appeared for the first time in the 1292 census of Paris.[2] In the thirteenth century Étienne Boileau, the provost to Paris, published a book of trades detailing the commercial life of the city. This oldest published document on the craftsmen of France also accorded the right to make mustard to the *vinaigriers*, who sold vinegar and vinegar-based sauces on the streets. According to the nineteenth-century French writer Alexandre Dumas, in thirteenth-century Paris the freshly prepared mustard sauces were sold at dinner time by specialized vendors, known as 'criers', who would run through the city streets, shouting 'mustard sauce'.[3]

By the fourteenth century, the manufacture of mustard in Dijon was governed by a decree and mustard had established its place at high tables. Guillaume Tirel, nicknamed Taillevent,

the cook of King Charles v of France, described in his book *Viandier*, published in 1390, a peculiar recipe for mustard sops – mustard poured over pieces of squared toast. Taillevent – literally 'cut wind' in French, meaning a light sail, which was in reference to his pronounced nose – was the first cook ever appointed to a king of France, and in that he became the first celebrity chef in Europe. Even though there seem to be doubts that he was involved at all in the writing of the book, this historically important publication shows what the French royalty ate in the Middle Ages.

Le Ménagier de Paris (The Parisian Household Book) was another book of this period where mustard recipes were included. This medieval guidebook described how a woman could run a prosperous household and maintain a proper

25

marriage in 1393. Besides gardening tips, domestic economy and even sexual advice, the book contained recipes. Written in the voice of an elderly husband addressing his younger wife, *Le Ménagier* introduced recipes for mustard, more as guidelines than precise descriptions, as was the norm in medieval cookbooks. Mustard is mentioned as a condiment for fish such as whiting, sole and sardines, but also for beef tongue and cow udders.

Another French city famous for its mustard is Meaux, built on the banks of Marne River about 40 kilometres (25 mi.) east of Paris, where mustard seeds were being milled the seventeenth century, with the millstones coming from local quarries. This hot and spicy mustard was prized by Jean Anthelme Brillat-Savarin, the French gastronome of the eighteenth and early nineteenth centuries: 'If it isn't Meaux, it isn't mustard!' Meaux is also famous for its Brie cheese and as the birthplace of Alexis Benoist Soyer, the French chef who became a celebrity cook in Victorian England. Throughout his eccentric career Soyer worked to improve the food of British soldiers and invented a gas stove, a refrigerator with cold water and ovens with temperature control. He also invented Soyer's relish, Soyer's sauces and Soyer's aromatic mustard, the latter defined as 'a most exquisite combination of the genuine mustard seed with various aromatic substances; infinitely superior to all other preparations of mustard'.[4] This mustard was so pungent that 'it caused the involuntary shedding of many a tear down the cheek of the gourmet'.[5]

In 1634, the Guild of Mustard Makers of Dijon regulated the production of mustard to ensure high standards and to keep away competition. Finally, in the eighteenth century, improvements in the milling of mustard seed were patented and the creation of the mustard known as *Moutarde de Dijon*, the Mustard of Dijon, was established. In this new patent verjuice (the tart and slightly fermented juice of unripe grapes) of Burgundy was added to brown mustard seeds and this mixture was milled using millstones, thus avoiding overheating this highly sensitive mustard paste.

Over centuries, mustard became more and more synonymous with refinement and pleasure. At the beginning of the nineteenth century, manufacturers competed with each other with their fine and aromatic mustards. When the industrial revolution first made its appearance in France around 1850, the manufacturing process of mustard became entirely mechanized. Maurice Grey invented a machine that automatized mustard production. His invention earned him a gold medal from the Académie des Sciences, Arts et Belles-Lettres of Dijon in 1853, and he became mustard supplier to Emperor Napoleon III in 1860. It was around this time, in 1866, that Grey Poupon was born as a brand of wholegrain mustard in Dijon under the ownership of Maurice Grey and Auguste Poupon. It would take another century before it became known as 'one of the finer things in life' in the New World.

It was the addition of verjuice that is said to have given Dijon mustard its distinctive qualities. The use of this 'green grape juice' (from Middle French *vertjus*) as an ingredient in sauces was common in the Middle Ages across Europe. It was a cooling condiment and its acidity counterbalanced the heat of spices. By the sixteenth century, Burgundy was already famous for its verjuice.

From the Middle Ages, the flavour quality of mustard made with verjuice was recognized. Furthermore, it was understood that acids present in the juice promoted the development of mustard essence and stabilized it. Verjuice could be made from a plump acidic grape called *bourdelas*, with large berries, as it was difficult for this grape to reach maturity and, even when it did so, it was too acidic for making

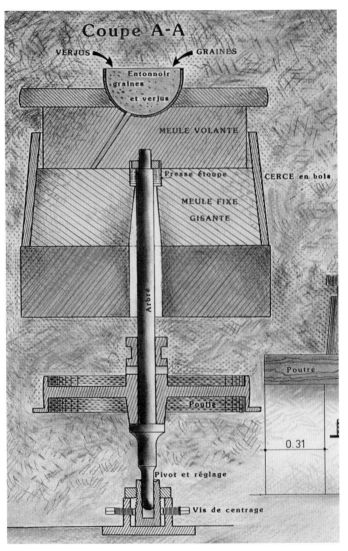

A sketch of the Maurice Grey mustard maker, 19th century.

wine. The other solution was to use regains or *conscrits*, grapes that were still too young to be picked at harvest time. In this case, any grape variety could be used. When the *phylloxera* insect epidemic hit the vineyards in Europe in the mid-nineteenth century, the *bourdelas* plant, which was more sensitive to *phylloxera* than the American plants, was replaced by the more noble grape varieties Chardonnay and Pinot Noir, intended for wine production. These grapes were also too noble for mustard, and so from that time on vinegar, instead of verjuice, was used for the manufacture of mustard in Burgundy.

Dijon mustard today is made from whole brown mustard seeds or a blend of several types of seeds, white wine vinegar and white wine, to imitate the verjuice in the historical recipe. The ingredients ferment in a tank for twelve hours before mixing, which gives it a strong flavour. Dijon mustard therefore takes longer to make than yellow mustard. It is also made with twice as many seeds and 20 per cent less water than yellow mustard and this makes it thicker and denser. For smooth and creamy Dijon and Burgundy mustard, the husks from crushed seeds are then filtered; for wholegrain mustard the seeds are left in.

Mustard was cultivated in charcoal burner clearings where charcoal kilns were located. Until the Second World War there were many charcoal kilns in the woodland-dense region of Burgundy. Discarded ashes from charcoal burning were rich in potash and encouraged the growth of mustard. Collectors would bring the seeds from the charcoal makers and sell it to mustard makers in Dijon. Mustard production in Dijon dwindled when the demand for coal diminished.

Today, there are no longer mustard manufacturers in Dijon and the method of manufacturing with a stone mill has almost totally disappeared. If you travel through France in

Children with a barrel of Dijon mustard, in a painting by François-Louis Lanfant De Metz, 19th century, oil on wood panel.

the spring you will see fields covered in yellow flowers. These flowers resemble mustard flowers but they are in fact rapeseed, with flowers very similar to the mustard plant. France imports nearly 90 percent of its mustard seeds from Canada. After a dispute in 1937, Dijon mustard was recognized as a recipe, conforming to certain ingredients and methods rather than a geographical production. Therefore the seeds and the production can come from outside the area.

Burgundians have always had the reputation of being fine gourmets and the people of Dijon were and still are known for their mustard making, although now on a much smaller scale. The mustard of Dijon has been a symbol of food elitism, and even sparked a political dispute in 2009 when former u.s. president Barack Obama was criticized by America's conservative media for having ordered a burger with Dijon mustard, instead of ketchup or any regular mustard. This entered the annals of mustard history as the 'Dijongate' scandal.

An important stage in Dijon mustard's history is found today in France on many bistro tables, where one almost always sees a bottle of Amora. This popular brand can be traced back to François Naigeon, *maître vinaigrier* of the eighteenth century, who became a 'Master Vinegar Maker' in 1703. Half a century later, Naigeon's son Jean-Baptiste introduced major changes to the manufacture of Dijon mustard and is credited for having first added grape juice or verjuice instead of vinegar and thus developed a secret way of preserving the mustard.

In the nineteenth century, the company passed through several successors and in 1919 ended up with the family business of Armand Bizouard, who registered the name Amora. It is said that under the spell of the taste of his mustard he exclaimed: 'It's a love of mustard, it will be Amora!' Raymond Sachot, the head of the company in the 1930s, was comforted in this choice when he discovered, on the occasion of an Egyptian temple visit, that Amora was the name of the god of the rising sun, Amon Ra. This discovery was further embraced in a marketing advertisement years later.

The 1930s saw the industrialization of production. Mustard was frequently used to promote health at this time and often appeared in French caricatures. In 1934, the glass jar replaced the original sandstone pot, marketed by the motto: 'There are no good mustards in ugly pots' (*Il n'est pas de bonnes moutardes dans de vilains pots*). By 1939, Amora was the number one producer of mustard in France, above Grey Poupon. After a pause in production during the Second World War, the company acquired others and grew further, dominating the market. One of these acquisitions was the Savora brand from Reckitt and Colman's. In the 1940s, Amora travelled all over France with hundreds of trucks carrying slogans such as 'Pas de bons repas sans Amora' (no good meal without

Advertisement for Amora mustard, 1961.

Amora). In 1953, the mustard jar of Amora evolved with the appearance of the reusable glass jar 'Givror', on the theme of cartoons, fables of La Fontaine or comics. Since the 1980s, Amora has extended its glass jar collection with licences from cartoons such as Spiderman, Smurfs and Nemo, and icons of cinema, such as Star Wars. With this particular promotion Amora has successfully became part of French life and remained an affordable condiment for everyday use, even after its acquisitions by big corporations: Danone and later Unilever.

The Maille name first became known in 1720 during an outbreak of plague, which decimated the population of southern France. Antoine Maille, a distiller and vinegar maker, supplied the people of Marseilles with an antiseptic vinegar that was claimed to prevent infection when rubbed on the body. He established the Maison de Maille and in 1747 opened his shop on the Rue St André des Arts in Paris. During the eighteenth century, mustard makers vied with one another to create new recipes and Antoine Maille was the most inventive of them all. He developed more than twenty varieties of mustard, flavoured with garlic, Chartreuse (a French herbal liquor), capers, nasturtium, tarragon and truffles. By the 1770s, Maille's success had brought appointments from the royal families of Austria, France, Hungary and Russia. After Antoine Maille died his son took over the business and in 1845 the first shop in Dijon was opened. His son,

Advertisement for Amora 'in a decorated glass jar', c. 1934.

34

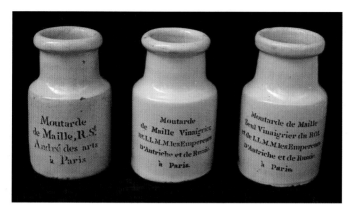

Stone pots from the French company Maille, 18th century.

Antoine-Claude Maille, enhanced his father's reputation and sold vinegars, mustards and condiments so successfully that he became the official supplier of vinegars and mustards to European kings and queens, including Louis xv of France. He developed a range of vinegars for hygiene and beauty: from skin care to hair care to gargling and bathing. With evocative names such as 'Vinegar of Venus', Maille's creations were a great success among aristocratic ladies throughout Europe. Following the death of the last surviving member of the Maille family in 1930, the company entered an era of expansion under several different owners.

After much expansion and many acquisitions Maille is still a luxury brand recognized in France and abroad, known for its original and wholegrain mustards and condiments containing exclusive ingredients. One can step into the Maille boutique in Dijon or Paris today and tap a jar of classic mustard *à la pompe* or buy a box of mustards flavoured with classic combinations, such as tarragon, honey or mayonnaise (which is called Dijonnaise) or with exotic ingredients such as champagne, cognac or black truffle. The decadent slogan of Maille, 'Il n'y a Maille qui m'aille', which more or less means 'only Maille suits me', is as valid today for this luxury brand as it has ever been. It is *the* Dijon mustard one finds in delicatessen shops all over the world.

Beyond the well-known brands, there have been attempts made over the years to reintroduce mustard cultivation in France. The renaissance of Burgundian mustard production came with the approval of a PGI (Protected Geographical Indication) label for 'mustard of Burgundy' (*moutarde de Bourgogne*). Since 2009, local producers have been able to use this label. Today only a few small, artisan family producers such as Téméraire, Renne de Dijon and Edmond Fallot are producing Burgundy mustard, which must include mustard seeds grown in Burgundy and at least 25 per cent Burgundy white wine (Aligoté and/or Chardonnay).

Edmond Fallot, a family company located in Beaune, Burgundy, since 1840, produces a Burgundy mustard from seeds grown in the region combined with Burgundy wine. Marc Désarménien, the current head of the company, is determined to modernize the company while keeping all its essential qualities, especially the use of millstones for slow mustard-seed crushing. Edmond Fallot continues to crush its seeds with millstones, which the company claims maintains a better flavour and strength.

Visitors to La Moutarderie Edmond Fallot can view the production, which consists of a hopper that receives the mustard seeds before they are crushed by a stone wheel. They can fill their fresh mustard pot at the 'mustard bar' with classics like Dijon mustard, wholegrain mustard or the Burgundy mustard, but also new recipes such as Pinot Noir mustard, basil Dijon mustard and gingerbread mustard.

For some years now, Fallot has produced verjuice from grapes picked before they have reached maturity. At the

'He knows . . . the little one', vintage Fallot advertisement.

Violet mustard, made with grape must, from Brive, France.

moment, it is not produced in sufficient quantities for the manufacture of mustard. The product is mainly used for cooking and chefs are bringing it back into fashion. In fact, Fallot has been recognized by the greatest chefs of France, including Paul Bocuse and Joël Robuchon.

The violet mustard from Brive, in the Limousin region in south-central France, is created from the mixture of seeds of mustard with black grape must, wine vinegar and spices. The black grape must imparts a violet hue and a fruity sweetness to the mustard. The addition of spices, including cinnamon and clove, gives it a complex flavour. One can use *moutarde violette* in almost any way other prepared mustard is used. In

Brive it is eaten with the famous Limousin beef, veal, duck, blood sausage or cold cuts. It is also excellent as an ingredient to flavour sauces and vinaigrettes.

Belgian Mustard

As mustard travelled from Dijon to England it made a culinary stop in the Lowlands. The Netherlands and Belgium produce various styles of mustard, such as Groningen mustard, Limburg mustard and Ghent mustard, often used as a dip, in sandwiches or in mustard soup. Tierenteyn in Ghent, Belgium, is a company that has been active in mustard production since 1818.

The first Tierenteyn to produce mustard in Ghent was Petrus Tierenteyn (1788–1857), who, according to legend, had overheard a conversation on the making of mustard between Napoleon and one of his soldiers. More likely Petrus started making mustard because the presence of the French in Ghent had created a demand for this condiment.

In the early days, the mustard was made by grinding the mustard seeds, vinegar and salt in a mortar. This was a very labour-intensive process which made the product rather expensive. In 1842, Petrus Tierenteyn managed to acquire a steam engine to facilitate the production of the mustard and made it affordable to a wider public. Because of this installation, the mustard shop became known as a *usine à vapeur* (steam factory).

Petrus had seven children and two of them continued the business: Ferdinand Tierenteyn and Augustus Franciscus Tierenteyn. Ferdinand founded his 'steam factory' and focused from the beginning on selling to wholesalers, while Augustus Franciscus was more interested in selling to consumers in his grocery shop. Both companies still exist today, having been taken over by other families, and continue to make mustard. The Antwerp-based author Willem Elsschot wrote a number of verses as publicity for Ferdinand Tierenteyn. These were published annually in *Snoecks Almanak* from 1949 until 1959, and later gathered in a small booklet.[6] The poems described how the best mustard came from Ferdinand Tierenteyn in Ghent:

Belgian mustard from Tierenteyn-Verlent in a stone pot.

Catherine Caesens, the current owner of Tierenteyn-Verlent, pouring mustard from a barrel.

De armste man en de rijkste vent
zijn zonder mosterd niet content.
Het beste eten is zonder smaak,
maar met mosterd is het een andere zaak

The poorest man and the richest guy
are not content without mustard.
The best food is without taste,
but with mustard it is a different matter.

The mustard of Franciscus Augustus under the Tierenteyn-Verlent name is still produced in the heart of Ghent, beneath the old shop at Groentenmarkt, selling directly to consumers.

The recipe is still very simple and includes only mustard seeds, vinegar and salt, with no additives or flavourings, so the product keeps for around a couple of months when refrigerated. The mustard is sharp, reminiscent of horseradish, has a smooth texture (or coarse with some mustard seeds), and is still poured from a wooden vat with a large wooden spoon into the glass or earthenware jars that the customers can buy in the shop or bring with them.

German Mustard

Known as *Senf* or *Mostrich*, German mustard is made with different varieties of ground mustard seeds mixed with vinegar, oil, herbs and/or sweeteners. It ranges from smooth to coarse-ground in texture, from pale yellow to brown in colour, and extra spicy to sweet in style. Düsseldorf mustard, with a sweet-sour taste, is one of the most famous German mustards. Düsseldorf is the city where the first mustard factory in Germany was built, in 1726. Particular to Düsseldorf mustard is the dish that it is served in, called a *Mostertpöttche*, an earthenware pot with painted blue letters, ABB, standing for Adam Bernhard Bergrath, the first producer. This beloved mustard jar was even immortalized in a well-known still-life painting by Vincent van Gogh. Van Gogh was giving painting lessons to amateur artists and he painted this picture while his pupils were busy with similar still-life paintings, not far from Düsseldorf.

Perhaps the most internationally famed German mustard is the sweet mustard from Bavaria, which is traditionally enjoyed with *Weisswurst*, white sausage, and is thus often described as *Weisswurstsenf* or white sausage mustard. Bavarian mustard and *Weisswurst* are to Oktoberfest are what yellow mustard and hot dogs are to American baseball games. The birth of *Weisswurst* mustard is attributed to Johann Conrad Develey in the nineteenth century in Munich. This business-man came from an old Huguenot family (de Veley) and had landed in Munich from French Switzerland via Lindau and Augsburg, where he completed his schooling. Develey started a mustard factory right in the centre of Munich. At that time in Munich, French-style medium and strong mustards were produced. Develey recognized very quickly that a sweet

Vincent van Gogh, *Still-life with Bottles and Earthenware*, November 1884–April 1885, oil on canvas.

Löwensenf extra-hot Düsseldorf mustard.

variation of mustard was missing from the market. In 1854, he added vinegar, sugar and spices to yellow and brown mustard for the first time and boiled the mixture. Later, the mustard grains were no longer boiled but instead ground, and brown icing sugar was added. With this final touch, the sweet mustard of Bavaria was born. This unique sweet mustard was awarded the Medal of Progress at the World Expos in Vienna in 1873 and Develey was named a purveyor to the court of King Ludwig II, making him a Royal Bavarian Court supplier.

Händlmaier Hausmachersenf, Bavarian sweet mustard.

English Mustard

Mustard is England's only commonly grown spice and is among the simplest foodstuffs on the British table. Its simplicity is central to its continuing appeal. Connoisseurs use mustard powder in cooking and ready-made mustard as a condiment. Mustard is traditionally served as an accompaniment to roast beef, but in its native East Anglia, where arable farming is more widespread than beef-rearing, mustard was more often served with game birds, rabbit and hare and, in coastal regions, with grilled herring. Although mustard cultivation is mainly concentrated in East Anglia, some mustard is also grown in Yorkshire and the Cotswolds.

The earliest appearance of mustard in a British cookbook dates back to one of the most influential cookbooks in medieval Europe, which was written by master cooks of King Richard II, in 1390, after *Le Viandier* and before *Le Ménagier de Paris* were published. It was a handwritten scroll called *The Forme of Cury*. The name of the recipe collection was given on the occasion of the publication of a later edition, in 1780, its title meaning 'the method of cooking', *cury* deriving from the Middle French *cuire*: to cook. The original fourteenth-century manuscript is today housed in the British Library. Some recipes in *The Forme of Cury* appear to be influenced by the medieval cookbook *Liber de coquina*, also published in the fourteenth century.

Mustard powder was not known in the UK until 1720. At that time, the seed was only coarsely pounded in a mortar and separated from its husk, and in that rough state prepared for use. *Delightes for Ladies*, a book of recipes and household tips for women, written by Sir Hugh Plat and published in London in 1602, mentions mustard flour in Venice as a novelty for England: 'It is usual in Venice to sell the meale of Mustard in their markets as we doe flower and meale in England: this meale, by the addition of vinegar, in two or three daies becommeth exceeding good mustard.'[7] *The English Housewife,* a book of English cookery and remedies published in 1615, gives a sauce recipe for wild fowl prepared with mustard and vinegar or mustard and verjuice. The book mentions another recipe for a mustard plaster.

The introduction of mustard flour in England is attributed to a woman named Mrs Clements, a resident of Durham. She is said to have ground mustard seeds in a mill in 1720, and obtained a superior fine powder, which came to be known as Durham mustard. It is said that she kept her secret for a long while and made a fortune with her mustard flour.[8] Later, when the processing of mustard seeds moved elsewhere, the name stayed.

On the other hand, Tewkesbury, in Gloucestershire in the west of England, was noted for its mustard balls. Legend has it that Tewkesbury Mustard Balls covered in gold leaf were presented to Henry VIII when he visited the town in 1535. The women of Tewkesbury used to gather the ingredients from the local fields and riverbanks. They would crush the mustard seeds to a flour in an iron mortar, and sieve the granules to produce a mustard sauce. They would then mix it with an infusion of horseradish, which was a common weed around Tewkesbury, form it into balls and allow them to dry on a board. The customer would then cut off as much as was required and steep it in water, milk, cider or cider vinegar until it was a 'thick and pungent' sauce. This was the form of mustard familiar to William Shakespeare when, in *Henry IV*, he had Falstaff describe Poins as having 'a wit as thick as Tewkesbury mustard' (II.4).

By 1662, Tewkesbury mustard was considered the best in England by Thomas Fuller, in *The History of the Worthies of England.*[9] In 1712 Sir Robert Atkins, in his *New History of Gloucestershire*, found Tewkesbury 'remarkable for making balls of the best Mustard'. 'He looks as if he lived on Tewkesbury mustard' came to be used as slang in Gloucestershire for those who always have a sad, severe and terrific expression. The manufacture of Tewkesbury mustard died out only at the beginning of the nineteenth century, perhaps coinciding with Mr Colman of Norwich inventing his new process for producing mustard flour.[10]

Until recently the mustard balls were made only to order and on special occasions such as the re-enactment of the Battle of Tewkesbury in July of each year. The tradition has now been restored, since 2013, by the Tewkesbury mustard company set up by Robin Ritchie and Samantha Ramsey, who make the mustard by hand using local ingredients according to the historical recipes – including mustard flour, finely grated horseradish root, white wine and honey – and sell it in both jars and ball format.

The legendary mustard of the UK is Colman's, being one of a few company names linked firmly to a single product. The legend of Colman's started at the Stoke Holy Cross Mill, to the west of Stoke Holy Cross village in south Norfolk, approximately 6.4 kilometres (4 mi.) south of Norwich. Jeremiah Colman took over a mustard flour business from Edward Ames based on the River Tas. From there, Colman's produced their very first mustard products in 1814. When Jeremiah Colman's adopted nephew James became his partner they called the firm J. & J. Colman. They opened a shop on London's Cannon Street in 1836 and moved the factory to Carrow in Norwich in 1854, starting with the mustard mill and eventually moving the whole business there by 1862. Stoke Mill still stands today and is now a restaurant with a display of Colman's memorabilia.

Colman's mustard tin, *c.* 1885.

While most mustards are prepared from wet milled seeds, English mustard is prepared from milled, dehusked mustard kernels. This makes it more concentrated than other mustards. First the husk is broken on rollers to release the kernels. Then the husk is separated from the kernel by using air. The kernel passes through rollers to mill it into a pure flour before it is packaged in the distinctive yellow tin of Colman's famous mustard powder.

In the beginning, mustard powder (fine, superfine or double superfine) was mostly packed in casks of 4 to 33 kilograms (9 to 72 lb) and sent to grocers who would then sell the powder to their customers in paper bags. Husks of mustard seeds were sold to farmers as manure, and oil extracted from the husks was sold as a lubricant. Only in the 1850s were Colman's recognizable yellow labels and decorated containers introduced. By the 1880s, mustard powder was available in 25 differently sized containers. The first pre-made mustard, which contained spices and vinegar, came much later when in 1899 Colman's introduced Savora mustard for export to France. Savora mustard – later bought by Amora – was inspired by the flavours of India and became an iconic French condiment over the years. England would have its own pre-made mustard in 1915, although the public remained in favour of the more pungent flavour of the freshly mixed mustard.

Mustard seed for Colman's was grown in eastern England, principally in Cambridgeshire, southern Lincolnshire and Norfolk, where Jeremiah Colman started his mustard business after years of flour-milling experience. Colman's originated the concept of contract farming in 1878. According to the English Mustard Growers (EMG) association, two varieties of mustard seed go into Colman's mustard: white and brown. It is said that English mustard was traditionally made with black and white seeds. After the war, brown seeds were planted with more manageable shorter plants.[11] The white mustard seed is named Gedney and the brown mustard seed Sutton, after local parishes. The seeds of white mustard add heat and the seeds of brown mustard contribute pungency to the Colman's mustard. Seeds are sown in March and April, the plants flower in June and harvesting takes place in September.

Throughout the nineteenth century, Colman's was the leading mustard brand in the UK. In 1866, they were granted a royal warrant as manufacturers to Queen Victoria. Even after the death of Jeremiah James in 1898, the company kept growing, bought out another mustard brand, Keen, in 1903 and in 1938 formed a conglomerate with Reckitt. It was bought by Unilever in 1995. Keen was later sold to McCormick, along with French's.

Colman's bull's head logo had first been used in 1855 and was produced by Sir Joseph Causton & Sons Ltd., a printers and stationery manufacturers based in Eastleigh. There is no record of who composed the original bull's head design and there is no evidence of common templates used over certain time periods. The logo has appeared in Colman's advertising in many variations.

In the nineteenth century, chop houses in Britain served mustard with beef and pork and Colman's exported British mustard all around the world. Colman's success lay partly in their insistence on quality, working with mustard growers and having their own agronomy department. They were also philanthropic towards their employees, who received hot meals and benefited from a lending library, a school for their children and the first industrial nurse in Britain. Colman's English Mustard still retains its royal warrant, supplying the household of Queen Elizabeth II. Other warrants included Napoleon III of France (1867), the Prince of Wales (1868) and Victor Emmanuel II of Italy (1869).

By the First World War, the poster was well established as a means of mass communication. During the 1920s and '30s, advertising became less conventional and more witty. The poster was a relatively inexpensive way to advertise. During the Second World War, newsprint was rationed, but after the war Colman's was able to re-establish its name by means of poster advertising. Posters designed for Colman's portrayed a variety of social classes. John Hassall in particular was an artist who produced remarkable work for Colman's, including the Klondyke posters, referring to the Klondike gold rush (the migration of 100,000 prospectors to the very cold Klondike region of the Yukon in northwestern Canada in

A Colman's coin made to celebrate the World's Fair of 1878 in Paris.

'To Klondyke', colour lithograph advertising Colman's by John Hassall, *c.* 1899.

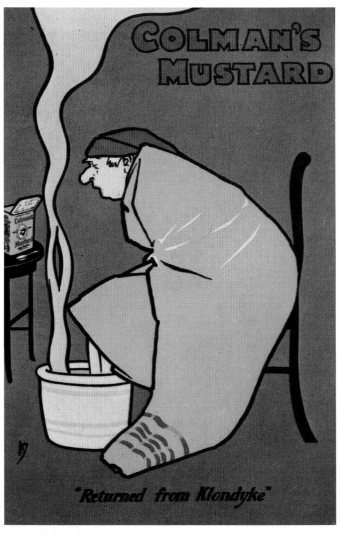

'Returned from Klondyke', Colman's advert by John Hassall, *c.* 1899.

1896–9). The posters of this period are criticized for not being aesthetically pleasing, but they were realistic and truthfully displayed the product image.

Colman's also excited the trade with its promotional items, much like biscuit and tea producers of the time. Every September, starting from 1880 for about six decades, 60,000 pictorial tins were ordered from tin printers for Christmas delivery. For special occasions additional alternative issues were made. For example, in July 1902 a tin was made to commemorate the coronation of King Edward VII and Queen Alexandra. In July of each year, an attractive card went out to the trade from the Cannon Street London Office describing the September tin of that year.

Early tins were decorated with scenes from the Empire, big game hunting, fish and flowers, and famous Victorian paintings. Patriotic themes continued into the twentieth century with British battleships, famous generals and national heroes. Famous places and buildings were also depicted. The tins held 1.8–2.7 kilograms (4–6 lb) of mustard and were of several different shapes: square, octagonal and rectangular, some with intricately curved corners. Later tins were made in more exotic forms, such as Crown Derby tubs and classic caskets. These tins were intended for grocers as well as large Victorian households. The mustard was put into bags made of greaseproof paper and each tin had an inner lid which was fastened down by little clips and sealed with the bull's head seal. The tins were designed with extensive after-use in mind, sometimes with a label declaring, 'This barrel will be found useful for storing sugar, tea, flour, rice etc.' These tins today are of increasing interest and value as collectors' items.

Between 1926 and 1933, the famous Mustard Club advertising campaign ran, created by Colman's in association with the advertising agency S. H. Benson. Posters appeared on

RULES *of the*
MUSTARD CLUB

1. **Every member** shall on all proper occasions eat Mustard to improve his appetite and strengthen his digestion.

2. **Every member** when physically exhausted or threatened with a cold, shall take refuge in a Mustard Bath.

3. **Every member shall once at least during every meal make the secret sign of the Mustard Club by placing the mustard pot six inches from his neighbour's plate.**

4. **Every member** who asks for a sandwich and finds that it contains no Mustard shall publicly refuse to eat same.

5. **Every member** shall see that the Mustard is freshly made, and no member shall tip a waiter who forgets to put Mustard on the table.

6. **Each member** shall instruct his children to " keep that schoolboy digestion " by forming the habit of eating Mustard.

The Password of the Mustard Club is
"Pass the Mustard, please."

Rules of the Mustard Club, from the Colman's advertising campaign, 1920s.

London buses asking 'Has Father Joined the Mustard Club?' Adverts in the press urged people to join. People were puzzled by the posters and rumours circulated; some people even rang the bus company and newspapers to find out what the Mustard Club was. The prospectus and the members of the club were also revealed: Baron de Beef of Porterhouse College, Cambridge; Miss Di Gester, secretary; Lord Bacon of The Rashers, Cookham; Signor Spaghetti, Parmesan Place, Stoke Doges; Lady Hearty, Tournedos Street, Mayfair; and Master Mustard, of Eaton, Bucks. Cartoons were released depicting these characters and their activities, and promotional items were sent out, including books, badges, mustard pots and card games. There were Mustard Club songs, books and fancy dress costumes. The crime writer Dorothy L. Sayers, who had worked for Bensons since 1922, was involved in the Mustard Club campaign. According to artist John Gilroy in an interview given in 1976, Sayers worked with him and William Brealey on the project, writing most of the copy and inspiring the cartoon characters.[12] A recipe book was produced which listed mustard as an ingredient in every recipe. The Mustard Club campaign was very successful. J. & J. Colman had to create a special office to deal with the work generated. At its peak, the Mustard Club received 2,000 applications requesting badges every day.[13]

From 1895 to 1953, Colman's produced a great number of small booklets for children as part of their wider advertising campaign. Most common were retellings of fairy stories and adaptations of great works of literature. In addition, there were informative and recreational booklets and illustrated lives of great historical figures. During the First and Second World Wars, the books were still printed, albeit in a smaller format. In the 1940s, a recurring set of characters called 'The Three Mustardeers', a trio of children reminiscent of those in the children's adventure novel series *The Famous Five* by Enid Blyton, began to feature in such adventures as *The Topsy Turvy Circus* (1946). The year 1950 saw *The Three Mustardeers and the League of the Zodiac*. Production of the booklets came to an end in 1953, as the amount of money allocated was no longer able to buy a sufficient quantity of booklets to provide a broad distribution.

Colman's had a mustard museum in Norwich until recently, which is closed at the time of the writing of this book, and expected to reopen in a new location.

Italian Mustard and Mostarda

Italians enjoy mustard in two ways: the classical mustard sauce which is called *senape*, from latin *sinapis*, and as *mostarda*, a sweet condiment made of candied fruits and mustard oil. Mostarda resembles Indian chutneys pickled with mustard seeds or mustard oil. It is found in various styles in many regions of northern Italy. The most famous one no doubt is the mostarda of Cremona, or *mostarda di frutta*, with its whole fruits. It blends the sharpness of mustard with the sweetness of fruit and sugar.

In Piedmont, mostarda is known as *cugnà*, a mixture of spiced fruits, and served with boiled meats. In Asti, mostarda is made of quince, walnuts and dried fruit and preserved in wine must without mustard seeds. *Mostarda mantovana*, of Mantua in Lombardy, uses a local apple called *campanina* and the fruit is usually preserved in sugar syrup. In Vicenza, Veneto, the speciality is the jam-like *mostarda vicentina* made with quinces. In Carpi, of the Emilia-Romagna region, it resembles a thick jam and has no spices. Tuscan mostarda is made with apples and pears and powdered white mustard. In

Mostarda di frutti cremona, a mustard-flavoured fruit preserve, by Sperlari.

Calabria and Sicily, the fruit is cooked and preserved in wine must with no mustard.[14]

According to Sperlari, a producer of mostarda since 1836, mostarda of Cremona dates back as far as 1397, when an apprentice inadvertently let a melon fall into a honey tub. However, Columella, the first-century Roman writer on agriculture, made the earliest distinction between mostarda and mustard in his *De re rustica*. He called mostarda *mustaceum* and used it for preserving meats, whereas he mentioned mustard as *sinapsis* and described how it accompanied boiled meats.

Combining sweet and salty ingredients was an example of the medieval balance of taste. Probably the first manuscript to give instructions for how to make mostarda was the fourteenth-century cookbook *Liber de coquina*. One recipe involves crushing mustard seeds or rocket seeds with anise and cumin in a mortar and adding cinnamon, sugar, vinegar, breadcrumbs and pepper. It is then mixed with hot broth, wine or vinegar.[15] In another recipe mostarda is described as being obtained by boiling must to reduce it by three-quarters. Mustard seeds are then added, and the mixture is ground and boiled. This can be kept for four months and served with meat or pork. This sauce can also be mixed with cinnamon, sugar, cloves, pepper and cardamom to make other differently spiced versions.[16] The use of fruits in mostarda was not mentioned in the *Liber de coquina*.

In the fifteenth century, mustard was prepared in Italy in many forms. Martino da Como gives a recipe of mustard in his *Libro de arte coquinaria* (The Art of Cooking) using wild mustard (the charlock mustard, *Sinapis arvensis*), almonds, verjuice or vinegar. He describes red or violet mustard containing cinnamon and sodden (boiled) wine. He also gives a recipe for mustard balls, which could be carried in pieces on horseback. Martino da Como thought that French mustard was inferior, as we see in one of his recipes: 'It is merely thinned with bitter or sodden wine. This is French mustard – for what it's worth.'[17]

Another fifteenth-century reference to mustard can be found in *Cuoco Napolotano*. The book describes the Italian mustard and a balled version to be used for trips, giving us a glimpse of Italian travelling customs of the time. This cookbook is critical of French mustard: 'It is distempered with only tart wine or must. This is the French mustard, with neither head nor feet.' Interestingly, this book mentions a hemp seed mustard recipe, where hemp seeds replace mustard seeds and are used along with blanched almonds, bread and meat broth, almond milk and sugar.[18]

Cristoforo di Messisbugo, the Italian Renaissance cook of the House of Este in Ferrara, gives recipes for mostarda in his book *Libro novo* in 1557, in which he advises those preparing princely feasts, providing detailed descriptions of the menus for his official banquets at the Este court. His mostarda contains cinnamon, ginger, cloves and mustard. A stronger version includes strong white vinegar and apples in quarters (instead of sugar).[19] It is in this version that we start seeing fruit being used as a source of sugar and a predecessor to the fruit mostarda of today.

Bartolomeo Scappi, in his work *Opera* in 1570, describes how to make sweet mostarda and suggests to use it to accompany many dishes, ranging from ox's head to grilled tripe, wild boar's head cooked in wine, blood sausages and fish such as boiled sturgeon and smoked pike.[20]

Montaigne, the French Renaissance writer, mentioned a delicious mostarda made with *mele cotonie*, or quince, which he had the chance to taste in Fornovo di Taro, Parma, during his trip through northern Italy in 1580–81, and another one made with apples and oranges in Fidenza.[21]

By the nineteenth century, the use of mostarda was well established in Italy. In the *Cucina teorico-pratica* (Theoretical and Practical Cooking) by the cook and writer Ippolito Cavalcanti, published in Naples in 1839, which is known for giving the first description of vermicelli pasta topped with tomatoes, we see the use of apples, orange skins, pounded cloves and cinnamon powder in a sieved and sugared smooth mostarda sauce made with the must of black Angelica grapes.[22]

In 1891, Pellegrino Artusi, who is credited for creating the national Italian cuisine with his cookbook, which included recipes from all regions, published a recipe for a Tuscan mostarda with a comment on mustard's ability to stimulate appetite and facilitate digestion. He also published other recipes where mostarda is used as an ingredient, such as fritters stuffed with mostarda.[23]

Mustard in the East

Ancient Romans learned many preservation techniques from their trading in the East. In India, chutney is prepared with fruit and mustard seed. In medieval Cairo, there was a recipe close to *mostarda di frutta* called *ṣifat khardal*, which is described as a fish sauce that consisted of whole jujubes and raisins pickled in a marinade made of pounded mustard seeds macerated in vinegar, filtered, mixed with syrup and subsequently enriched with a rich spice mixture (*atraf at-tıb*), saffron and almonds. This sauce would be served on fried or cooked fish, unlike the mostarda of Cremona, which is used on roasted and boiled meat. This was an unusual sauce because in the Arabic-Islamic world whole fruits would not ordinarily be served as a fish sauce. This might have been an influence from the Italian peninsula.[24]

Mustard seems to have been quite appreciated in medieval Cairo. It was always on the table, in the form of both sauces and dips, such as mustard vinegar relish (*khall wa-khardal*), a paste made of crushed almonds moistened with vinegar to which ground mustard and some spices were added. There were also some unique mustard recipes with no equivalent in Roman cuisine. For example, halum cheese with sauce, a dish of unripened salted white cheese macerated in a sauce made of mustard, vinegar, a rich collection of herbs and spices, garlic crushed with olive oil, salt, nuts and tahini. Another unique recipe was mustarded eggs (*bayd mukhardal*). It was a snack made by covering boiled eggs with salt and cumin in the morning and seasoning them with saffron, vinegar, mustard seeds, mint and spice mix (*atraf at-tib*) in the evening.[25]

Mustard was recognized as a heating substance in the Persian-Arabic traditional medicine Yunani, practised in Mughal India and among Muslims in Central and South Asia. This medicine was based on the teaching of Greek physicians Galen and Hippocrates and developed by Ibn Sina (Avicenna). It included influences from the classical four humours as well as Indian and Chinese medicine. In Ibn Sina's *The Canon of Medicine*, from the eleventh century, mustard was mentioned as a pot herb that increased the amount of bile or excited the flow of bile. Because of its heating properties, any food containing mustard would enable travellers to endure exposure to cold more easily.[26]

Since the fifteenth century, a mixture of vinegar and crushed mustard seeds has been consumed with meats in Ottoman cuisine, perhaps inherited from Byzantium. Hans Dernschwam, a Bohemian merchant who visited Istanbul in the sixteenth century, wrote in his diary that the Turkish put mustard sauce on mutton.

Around the same time in Istanbul there was a fermented drink produced from grape juice, crushed mustard seeds and sour cherry leaves. This was an indigenous drink of the Thrace region in the northwest of Turkey called *hardaliye*, a name derived from *hardal*, mustard in Turkish.

In *The Turkish Letters*, Ogier Ghiselin de Busbecq, a Flemish diplomat, wrote that *hardaliye* was sold in Istanbul in the 1500s:

> They first place a layer of crushed mustard seeds in a clay pot or a wooden barrel, then place grapes above this, followed by another layer of mustard flour and press them tightly. When the barrel is nearly full with grapes they pour grape juice over them and seal the barrel. When hot days arrive and there is a lack of water they open these barrels and sell the grapes and its juice.[27]

Evliya Çelebi, an Ottoman explorer of the seventeenth century, also mentions *hardaliye* being consumed in Thrace in his *Seyathatname*. While the Greeks and Jews in the region were using grapes for wine production, Muslims were transferring grapes into other non-alcoholic products such as molasses, dried fruit pulp (*pekmez*) and *hardaliye*. Today *hardaliye* is embraced as a traditional drink of Thrace, produced in the region and distributed in Turkey. It pairs exceptionally well with the meatballs and fried liver of Thrace.

Kasundi is a sinus-clearing sauce of Bengali cuisine. It is made with fermented dry and ground mustard seeds, with or without mustard oil. Some families prepare *kasundi* with other spices or use it to make tomato *kasundi* or mango *kasundi*.

It was originally used as a type of *achar* (chutney or pickle) and was traditionally eaten with rice, greens and deep-fried foods. It was made by the Brahmin caste following rituals.

Only women who adhered to purity standards could make it. For example, women involved in its making could not be widows, or menstruating. They were not allowed to eat any bitter or sour food. *Kasundi* was not made in the month of a birth or the year of a death in the family, or if some tragedy had occurred to them in the past while making *kasundi*. In modern times, it is possible to find commercially available *kasundi* and it is popularly served with snacks like fried cutlets.

Karashi is Japanese yellow mustard and a popular sharp wasabi-like condiment in powder or paste form, traditionally served as a spicy dip with savoury dishes such as the fried breaded pork cutlet *tonkatsu*, the fermented soybean dish *natto*, the Chinese-style dumplings *shumai* and *oden* hot pot, or combined with miso paste and vinegar to create a tangy sauce called *karashi sumiso*. *Karashi* has a very hot and spicy taste because it is not mixed with vinegar. It is also the indispensable ingredient in one of Kumamoto's regional foods,

Karashi renkon (sliced lotus root filled with mustard and miso).

karashi renkon (lotus root filled with a mustard–miso paste and deep-fried), often enjoyed with sake.

American Mustard

European explorers, fishermen and traders often visited the shores of New England long before more significant and stable settlements were established there, in the middle of the seventeenth century. These early encounters formed the initial impression on both sides, including early impressions on how each liked a different kind of mustard.

When it comes to exploring and settling in North America, the English were a bit behind other European superpowers, the Spanish and the French in particular. The first important English explorer was Bartholomew Gosnold, who visited Cape Cod and the Martha's Vineyard area in 1602. Native Americans showed huge interest in European goods and traded some for skins. Mustard was one of the European goods exchanged. As John Brereton, the chronicler of the expedition, remarked: 'They misliked nothing but our mustard, whereat they made many a soure face,'[28] a testimony to the British taste for sharp mustard.

Although Lewis and Clark's expedition journals reported having seen Native Americans growing mustard on the south side of the Missouri river, in 1805–6, it is not clear to which species of mustard they refer, as *Brassica* species were brought to America in a later era.[29]

In the nineteenth century in America the use of mustard and other condiments was rising. Their adversaries followed. Food reformers believed that mustard was too exciting, and caused a variety of illnesses. The fashionable disease of the era was dyspepsia (indigestion). Many food reformers were in

The classic mustard hot dog.

accord with Christian theology, and mustard was up there with other dangers of intemperance: gluttony, meat, pepper, white bread and sexual indulgence. A number of self-educated 'doctors', most influential among them Sylvester Graham, a Presbyterian minister, promoted vegetarianism and lack of dietary stimulation. Graham's diet saw gluttony as the greatest of all causes of evil and banned meat, condiments, tea and coffee, sugars, spirits, drugs and tobacco.

According to Graham, mustard, pepper, ginger and, in short, all stimulating and heating spices and condiments were not only unnecessary but decidedly dangerous to organs and the whole body, retarding digestion and causing irritation to the stomach and inflammation in the mucous membrane of alimentary and respiratory cavities. He referred to a study by Dr William Beaumont, a surgeon of the U.S. Army who specialized in gastric physiology:

> He found that when mustard and pepper were taken with the food, they remained in the gastric cavity till all the food was digested, and continued to emit a strong aromatic odor to the last: and that the mucous surface

of the stomach presented a slight morbid appearance towards the close of chymification.[30]

Graham's objection to condiments was a theme for nineteenth-century America. Dr William Alcott, a prominent physician, campaigned against condiments. Dio Lewis, a Harvard-trained physician, announced: 'Everything which inflames one appetite is likely to arouse the other also. Pepper, mustard, ketchup and Worchester [*sic*] sauce – shun them all. And even salt, in any but the smallest quantity, is objectionable; it is such a goad toward carnalism.'[31]

Graham influenced other physicians of the late nineteenth century, such as John Harvey Kellogg and Charles W. Post, who promoted vegetarianism and their own grain-based products. Although the use of mustard and other condiments continued to grow in the twentieth century, Graham's ideas remain a part of the teachings of the Seventh-day Adventist Church today. They believe that 'Condiments are injurious in their nature. Mustard, pepper, spices, and pickles irritate the stomach and make the blood feverish and impure.'[32] The danger of these foods is seen in their stimulating character – that soon ordinary food does not satisfy the appetite and the body wants something more exciting.

The first American mustard was a ready-to-use dark spicy brown mustard produced by Gulden's in 1867. It is no coincidence that this was also the time hot dogs were first seen on the streets of New York and several other parts of the United States, after German immigrants arrived with their sausage culture in the 1850s. Gulden's mustard won its first award from the American Institute of the City of New York in 1869 for the product's fine flavour and for the technological advancements the company made; they were recognized for producing a mustard locally using American seeds while representing French and German flavours. Awards from the World's Columbian Exposition in Chicago (1893) and the Exposition Universelle in Paris (1900) followed.[33]

Charles Gulden gained various patents on containers for mustard, including a bulb-shaped mustard bottle, a squeeze bottle, a mustard jar cap and a mustard dispenser. His mustard recipe had simple ingredients: mustard seed, vinegar, spices and salt. After the success of the more bright-coloured French's mustard he would begin marketing Gulden's Prepared Yellow Mustard, coloured with turmeric, in 1949. Over the years other recipes were launched, but Gulden's spicy brown mustard was the only one that survived. Gulden's remains America's third most popular mustard, after French's and Grey Poupon, and holds the title of being the longest continuously produced mustard in the country.

Detail from a Gulden's letterhead, 1909.

French's mustard was created when one of the sons of a spice trader named Robert Timothy French, Francis, lobbied for a new kind of prepared mustard that was more pleasing to the changing American palate of the early twentieth century. The R. T. French Company had been founded in Rochester, New York, in 1880, manufacturing mustards, spices, flavouring extracts, prepared food mixes, household supplies and pet foods. George Dunn, the spice mill manager at their location at 1 Mustard Street in Rochester, was given the task of creating a new recipe. He stepped up to the challenge and developed a smooth, bright yellow and mildly flavoured mustard, distinctly different from the spicy mustards of the time. It was French's Cream Salad Brand Mustard. It sold in 255-gram (9-oz.) jars for ten cents and each jar came with a serving paddle.[34]

The French brothers brought their mustard to the 1904 World's Fair in St Louis for people to view and taste. The birth of the all-American mustard was witnessed by nearly 20 million visitors. It was served with hot dogs and became a big hit, doubling the sales of the French Company within five years. Hence French's is reportedly the first mustard to have been used as a hot dog condiment.

Ever since, according to many, French's mustard has been the best condiment to eat with hot dogs, especially in sports stadiums. The famous pennant on French's logo, introduced in 1915, was designed to resemble the pennants that fly over baseball stadiums. Since the year 2000, French's has been the official mustard of Yankee Stadium and it can be found in ballparks and stadiums around the country. After 1926, the French brothers sold their company to J. J. Colman, which changed to Reckitt & Colman and Reckitt Benckiser after mergers (in 1938 and 1999), and finally it was sold to McCormick in 2017.

French's Classic
Yellow Mustard.

After 1921, national advertisements helped French's to become a million-dollar business. French's introduced the 'Hot Dan the Mustard Man' advertising campaign in 1932 and began attaching Hot Dan spoons to jars of their mustard. Hot Dan was a potato-shaped man with curly hair and a big bow tie. The campaign continued to be the keystone of French's advertising until it was phased out in the 1940s. The spoons became a hot item for collectors, as well as for many mothers who claimed that this spoon was the best thing they could find for feeding their babies. French's adverts focused on how inferior mustard could ruin good ham or rich cheese, and showed how women could fix salmon, salads or burgers with French's tangy and zesty mustard instead. Although Hot Dan has disappeared from advertisements, French's mustard remains the number one most popular mustard in America, with an essentially unchanged recipe still sold in its iconic yellow squeeze bottle.

In 1946, the American company Heublein acquired Grey Poupon in France and placed this European mustard in the American market, which was dominated by French's. French's mustard was made from ground yellow mustard seeds and vinegar, coloured bright yellow with turmeric; Grey Poupon, by comparison, had a very French name and was made with white wine vinegar. Heublein saw the opportunity to promote Grey Poupon as a fine, premium product in a glass jar straight from Dijon, with a white cap like a flat french hat lined with the colours of the French flag. It worked. Americans grew to love Grey Poupon from its advertisements in the 1980s, one of which shows a Rolls-Royce pulling up alongside another car, and a passenger in one asks 'Pardon me, would you have any Grey Poupon?' The other responds, 'But of course!' and a Grey Poupon jar is passed between the two cars. This advertisement was later much parodied in other adverts, films and cartoons.

Heublein made the mustard in Hartford, Connecticut, until 1975, when it moved production to Oxnard, California. Then, in 1982, it merged with R. J. Reynolds. Nabisco joined R. J. Reynolds in 1985, and the Nabisco division of Reynolds

French's Hot Dan the Mustard Man.

has been making Grey Poupon ever since. Grey Poupon in France was bought by an even older brand, Maille, and it can still be purchased in the Maille boutique on the rue de la Liberté in the arterial street of Dijon.

The expensive French mustard with white wine vinegar remains the epitome of the finer things in life, and a symbol of sophistication. This and the fact that it rhymes with many words, such as futon, coupon and crouton, has made Grey Poupon a popular phrase, used in hundreds of hip-hop songs since the 1990s by many popular artists such as Das EFX, Justin Bieber and Kanye West.

Also in the U.S., mustard enthusiasts can visit a museum in Middleton, Wisconsin, that holds a collection of mustards from around the world and spreads the love for mustard by hosting 35,000 visitors a year, a worldwide mustard competition and other events. The National Mustard Museum was founded by Barry Levenson, a lawyer by trade, when his beloved Boston Red Sox lost the World Series, in 1986, and he decided to begin collecting jars of mustard to get over his depression. His hobby turned into an obsession and his job title to the curator and CMO – Chief Mustard Officer – of the museum. At the time of writing, the museum has hosted more than 60,031 types of mustard, mostly from across Europe, North America and Latin America, with quite a few from Asia and even some from Africa. In the museum there is a large display of mustard tins and jars, mustard as medicine and mustard-related art.

The iconic Grey Poupon jar.

Curtiss Mustard advertisement on a box of Butterfingers (a chocolate and peanut butter bar) from 1948.

The National Mustard Museum celebrates National Mustard Day every year on the first Saturday in August. The event traditionally includes games, music and other entertainment, with mustard sampling, bratwurst, hot dogs and more. The museum also doubles as an institute of higher learning with the mustard college known as the Poupon U. And while you cannot take any classes for academic credit at Poupon U, you can join in and sing their song:

> On our hot dogs, on our bratwurst, mustard is so cool.
> Never mayo, never ketchup; they're against the rules.
> Gleaming gold and mellow yellow; smooth, rough,
>   sweet and hot,
> Fight, POUPON U! We'll fight and eat some lunch.

Levenson is now developing a card game for mustard pairing. Levenson's personal favourite is the walnut mustard from

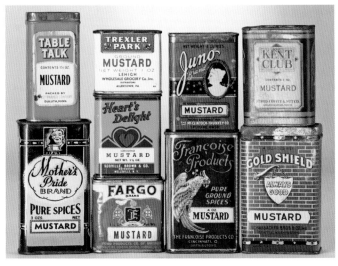

Vintage tins at the National Mustard Museum in Middleton, Wisconsin.

'Oh Barry . . . we're out of mustard', Pop art painting made for Barry Levenson, the founder of the National Mustard Museum.

Edmond Fallot in Beaune, where he visited and observed mustard production many years ago. In the museum shop one can sample mustards and buy one of the three hundred different mustards on sale.[35] He must be the only person in the world who will never run out of mustard.

3
Mustard in Language and Literature

Not surprisingly, mustard is a simile for sharpness, strength and impenetrability in many languages. 'As strong as mustard', 'as sharp as if he lived on Tewkesbury mustard', or 'as thick as Tewkesbury mustard', are a few examples from the English language. To be as 'keen as mustard' means to be very eager and enthusiastic – the expression, often thought to have originated with the company Keen & Sons' mustard, actually pre-dates it. Keen is used here to mean 'operating on the senses like a sharp instrument'.[1]

Mustard idioms are plenty. 'To cut the mustard' is to reach expectations.[2] 'A hot shot in a mustard pot (when both his heels stand right up)' means one who shoots eagerly with a firearm. 'To grind mustard with one's knees' is having knock-knees. Such a person is also called a 'Durham man', referring to the mustard powder of Durham. 'Moonshine in a mustard pot' is an expression from around the seventeenth century and means 'nothing'. Accordingly, 'to give moonshine in a mustard pot' is to give nothing.[3] 'As a cat loves mustard' or 'to love as a cat loves mustard' is an English proverb meaning to love something even if it is bad for you.[4]

In the political satire *Knights* by the ancient Greek poet Aristophanes, the sausage-seller describes the Council

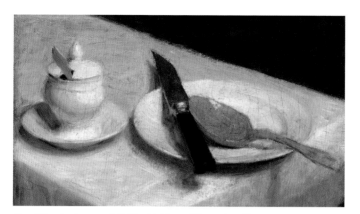

Henri Fantin-Latour, *Still-life with Mustard Pot*, 1860, oil on canvas.

(governing body of Athens) upon hearing slanderous allegations: 'as they were hearing this, the whole Council became full of false-orach, looked mustard and knit its brows'. Aristophanes here combines vision and taste.[5] The sensory experience of tasting and smelling mustard is figuratively transformed to looking. We can imagine the look to be rather sharp.[5]

In French, one can express that one is very angry by saying 'la moutarde me monte au nez', literally meaning 'the mustard goes up my nose'. 'Se croire le premier moutardier du pape' is another saying in France, which can be translated as 'to think of himself as the mustard maker of the pope'. It means to have a high opinion of oneself. It is said that Pope John XXII (1249–1334) loved mustard so much that he created a new position in the Vatican, the *Grand Moutardier du Pape*, Mustard-maker to the Pope.

Alexandre Dumas, in his *Grand Dictionnaire de Cuisine*, wrote:

> Among the Popes who held such a brilliant court in
> Avignon, Pope John XXII was one of those who did not

disdain the pleasures of the table. He loved mustard, put in everything, and not knowing what to do with one of his nephews who was good for nothing, he made him first mustard officer.

Hence comes the habit of saying of a vain fool that he thinks himself the first mustard maker of the pope. This expression was described for the first time in the *Dictionary of Trévoux* of 1771. This anecdote surfaced in the dictionaries of the nineteenth century, until the day the French lexicographer Émile Littré settled the question: 'There is no mustard maker among the officers of the Pope.'

In German, adding one's mustard (*seinen Senf dazugeben*) means the same as giving one's two cents in American English, one's humble opinion, or to intrude on a conversation. In Dutch, 'pulling or dragging someone through the mustard' (*iemand door den mosterd halen of sleepen*), means to displease someone. When Dutch people turn fifty they are said to be either 'seeing Abraham' or 'seeing Sarah', a reference to a verse in the Bible (John 8:57: 'You are not yet fifty years old,' they said to him, 'and you have seen Abraham!') and they get a pot of mustard as a present. Although the exact origin of this gesture is not known, it seems to signify that one knows 'where to get the mustard', that is, 'how life works' at this age. In Romanian, it is said of a person who loses his temper that his or her 'mustard will jump off' (*Îi sare muştarul*).

Mustard in Religious Literature

The tiniest seed of the mustard plant is loaded with flavour. So, too, do the fables of religious and secular literature imbue the seed with greatness.

French postcard titled 'Spices: Mustard', by Manuel H. (photographer), *c.* 1905.

In Buddhist teachings, mustard seed is used as a notable symbol. In ancient India, mustard was a common household commodity and its seed was considered a magical substance that could help counteract obstacles in life. In both the Hindu and Buddhist tantric traditions, mustard seed (*sarshapa* in Sanskrit) could be used in rites against all negative influences. *Sarshaparuna* (literally meaning the red mustard demon) is the name given to a certain spirit that possesses children, potentially referring to scarlet fever.[6]

The Buddhist text *Kisa Gotami and the Mustard Seed* teaches how death is a part of life. Kisa Gotami was the wife of a rich man in the ancient city of Savatthi in northern India. She experienced great sorrow after losing her only child and was taken to the Buddha. The Buddha told her that he could bring her child back if she could get a white mustard seed from a family which has had no death. After searching house after house Kisa Gotami saw that every house had mustard seed but no house was spared from death. Having learned a lesson about death, Kisa Gotami returned to the Buddha enlightened and accepting of her loss.[7]

In Jewish texts the universe is compared to a mustard seed to demonstrate that all that exists now was packed into the tiniest imaginable speck of space at the universe's beginning. Nahmanides, a medieval Jewish scholar of the thirteenth century, described the universe as having expanded from the time of its creation, at which time it was the size of a mustard seed: 'At the briefest instant following creation all the matter of the universe was concentrated in a very small place, no larger than a grain of mustard.'[8]

The Bible uses the black mustard seed as a symbol of large growth from small beginnings in the Parable of the Mustard Seed, which appears in Matthew 13:31–2:

> He set another parable before them, saying, 'The Kingdom of Heaven is like a grain of mustard seed, which a man took, and sowed in his field; which indeed is smaller than all seeds. But when it is grown, it is greater than the herbs, and becomes a tree, so that the birds of the air come and lodge in its branches.'

The same metaphor also appears in Mark 4:30–32 and Luke 13:18–19 and in the non-canonical Gospel of Thomas (verse 20). The minuteness of the grain came to symbolize small beginnings. In the stories, because the seed is hot when it has been crushed, it is attractive to birds that are drawn to the plant for food and shelter. As mustard in reality does not grow into a tree and mustard plant does not attract nesting birds, a plant becoming a tree might suggest an expansion beyond its nature. The birds are generally interpreted as converts coming to Christianity, but others have interpreted them as satanic creatures invading the Church.[9] In any case, the choice of mustard seed is very interesting as it is neither the smallest seed on earth nor does it grow into a tree. Mustard is more like a bush. As Pliny the Elder writes: 'It grows entirely wild, though it is improved by being transplanted: but on the other hand when it has once been sown it is scarcely possible to get the place free of it, as the seed when it falls germinates at once.'[10] So it is probable that the biblical significance of mustard in this parable is its hardiness and resilience.

In Matthew 17:20 we find mustard seed representing faith.

> He replied, 'Because you have so little faith. Truly I tell you, if you have faith as small as a mustard seed, you can say to this mountain, "Move from here to there," and it will move. Nothing will be impossible for you.'

Christ tells an apostle how a mustard seed grows into a tree,
etching by Jan Luyken, late 17th century.

Today it is possible to buy a single mustard seed embedded in
a glass necklace as a sign of one's faith.

It is said that Christians carried mustard seeds and scattered them as they walked so mustard plants grew along their
pilgrimage trails. One of the places is a Bible trail in California, supposedly visible from space when its yellow flowers
are in bloom. The city of Gonzales in Monterey County,
California, has a trail marker and a mural to celebrate the
mustard seed trail.

The legend of 'the mustard seed trail' is rooted in the
Portolà expedition, which travelled through the Ohlone tribal
lands carrying sacks of mustard seeds. These seeds were
spread behind them as they travelled north in the winter,
marking a trail for their return in the spring by a blooming
yellow pathway. The Portolà was the first recorded Spanish
(or any European) land entry and exploration of the present-
day state of California, in 1769–70. The expedition was led
by Gaspar de Portolà, who became the first governor of

California. Three groups travelled by sea, while two other groups travelled by land on mule trains.

Portolà's path would later be called El Camino Real (The King's Road), a 1,125 kilometre (700-mi.) footpath that ran along the coast from San Diego to Sonoma, connecting 21 missions founded by Franciscans. Many claim that Franciscans sowed mustard seeds along the primitive route to mark the way for travellers. It is said that grape vines were planted on the same trail, and therefore mustard plants are seen along the vineyards in California, from San Diego to Sonoma. Each spring mustard plants bloom in bright yellow along much of U.S. Route 101, which traces the Old Camino trail.

It is not possible to prove this story true or false as mustard might have been spread along the route before the Franciscans arrived. Juan Crespí, the chronicler of the Portolà expedition of 1769, was struck by the fact that grasslands had recently been burned down by the local inhabitants. But there is no mention of the expedition sowing mustard seeds then. Another theory is that mustard seeds travelled from Spain by accident, on the livestock Juan Bautista Anza brought to southern California with the first colonists in 1775.

What is known is that the Spanish introduced plants into this area, most notably wild oats and mustard, which dominated coastal pasture by 1900. Wildflowers, filaree and clover were in the interior instead. In the 1920s, the inland pastures of Riverside and San Bernardino were further transformed and dominated by wild oat and mustard fields. [11]

Mustard seed is also to be found in the Quran, referring to something small in weight, to represent the justice that will be brought forth by Allah. 'None shall enter the Fire (of Hell) who has in his heart the weight of a mustard seed of Iman [faith] and none shall enter Paradise who has in his heart the weight of a mustard seed of pride.' [12]

Mustard in Secular Literature

In secular literature and customs, reference to mustard is plentiful. In the sixteenth century, François Rabelais wrote novels that told of the extravagant adventures of two giants, Gargantua and his son Pantagruel. One story describes how Gargantua was fed with shovelfuls of mustard by four men on his shoulders at a dinner hosted by the king of Paris, as a way to treat his phlegm and indigestion:

> and because he was naturally phlegmatic, he began his meal with some dozens of gammons, dried neats' tongues, hard roes of mullet, called botargos, andouilles or sausages, and such other forerunners of wine. In the meanwhile, four of his folks did cast into his mouth one after another continually mustard by whole shovelfuls.[13]

The image of Gargantua was used as a symbol of *gourmandise*, appreciation of good food, by the mustard producer

Detail from Rabelais' *Gargantua and Pantagruel* by Gustave Doré, 1873.

A poster for Charles Dumont Dijon mustard, chromolithograph, *c.* 1910.

Charles Dumont in an advertisement in the early twentieth century.

The same book also described the meals of friars on the island of Sandals, though the foods appeared in the opposite order: cheese first, then puddings and sausages and all types of meat, and finally mustard and lettuce, as the ancients ate them, and thus they made good the proverb 'after meat comes mustard'. We still use the idiom 'after meat, mustard', which means doing something in the wrong order, as mustard was supposed to come before meat.

In Shakespeare's *A Midsummer Night's Dream*, 'Mustard-seed' is the name of one of the four servants of Titania, the fairy queen, next to Peaseblossom, Cobweb and Moth. In *Macbeth*, the brave, eponymous Scottish general receives a prophecy from a trio of witches that one day he will become king of Scotland. As they stir their boiling cauldron, the Second Witch gives the recipe for their witchery.

Fillet of a fenny snake,
In the cauldron boil and bake;
Eye of newt and toe of frog,
Wool of bat and tongue of dog,
Adder's fork and blind-worm's sting,
Lizard's leg and howlet's wing,
For a charm of powerful trouble,
Like a hell-broth boil and bubble. (IV.I)

The eye of newt boiling and baking in the cauldron of witches in *Macbeth* is no other than the brown mustard seed.

In Shakespeare's *Taming of the Shrew*, the following dialogue takes place between Petruchio's servant Grumio and the quick-witted, sharp-tongued Katherina of Padua, who is being starved by her husband Petruchio (who arrives late for his wedding, badly dressed, behaves poorly during the service, does not stay for the reception and takes her back to his country house, where he refuses to let her eat, sleep or dress well until she conforms to his every whim).

GRUMIO

What say you to a piece of beef, and mustard?

KATHERINE

A dish that I do love to feed upon.

GRUMIO

Ay, but the mustard is too hot a little.

KATHERINE

Why then, the beef, and let the mustard rest.

GRUMIO

Nay then, I will not. You shall have the mustard
Or else you get no beef of Grumio.

KATHERINE

Then both, or one, or anything thou wilt.

GRUMIO

Why then, the mustard without the beef.

KATHERINE

Go, get thee gone, thou false deluding slave,

Beats him

That feed'st me with the very name of meat.

Sorrow on thee and all the pack of you,

That triumph thus upon my misery.

Go, get thee gone, I say. (IV.3)

The many meanings that were given to mustard in religion, literature and idioms illustrate how mustard came to be a symbol of character and a metaphor for strength, small beginnings, growth, faith and enthusiasm. No other plant can spice up our food, our language and our literature as mustard does.

Hanging scroll of mustard plant and butterflies, from the early or middle Ming Dynasty (15th–16th century).

4
Mustard in Myths
and Medicine

In many cultures, mustard was believed to have numerous stimulating benefits, and as such it was a source of inspiration for various myths around the world. Pliny the Elder mentioned mustard as a cure for lethargy in women. According to German folklore, mustard seeds sewn into the hem of a bride's wedding gown will bring her power in the family. In Bengal and northern India, mustard seeds and salt are mixed together, waved around the head of a patient and then thrown into a fire, to ward off evil spirits. Mustard seeds were also thought to protect newborn babies and pregnant women in India.[1] Both in ancient China and medieval Europe, mustard was seen as an aphrodisiac because it increased blood circulation.

From the very early times of civilization, mustard was used as medicine. An ancient Sumerian clay tablet in cuneiform, dated to around 2100 BC, contains the world's oldest known prescription for mustard:

> Sift and knead together, all in one turtle-shell, the sprouting naga plant, salt and mustard; wash the sick spot with quality beer and hot water; scrub the sick spot with all of it (the kneaded mixture); after scrubbing rub with vegetable oil and cover with pulverized fir.[2]

Tin-glazed earthenware drug jar used for mustard, Sicilian, 17th century.

According to Chinese medicine, mustard promotes energy circulation, warms the body and removes phlegm. The proportion of yin (the female principle, passive and dark) and yang (the male principle, active and light) could be balanced by regulating food intake. Still today in China mustard seeds are used to treat colds, stomach problems and rheumatism. Within Ayurvedic medicine, found in sacred Indian writings called Vedas, the body is said to contain three elementary substances: spirit, phlegm and bile. Mustard is a stimulant; it regulates the metabolism, reduces mucus and promotes digestion.

An ancient belief in Europe, too, was that mustard stimulated the appetite, strengthened the stomach and facilitated digestion. Pythagoras stated that mustard seed occupied the first rank among alimentary substances, which exercise a prompt influence on the brain. As noted in the Introduction, it was believed that food had a direct effect on our humours, as particular combinations of food could help support a balanced, healthy body. Some spices, such as pepper, cinnamon and mustard, were considered hot and dry and were used as the basis for medicines and poultices. According to the Greek physician Hippocrates, mustard was 'hot and passed well by stool and hardly by urine'.[3] Hot and dry mustard counteracted cold conditions. As such, it was considered useful for digestion, for the lungs and against chronic coughs, sneezing and phlegm. It was used as a rub for muscle pain. In addition, mustard was believed to be medicinal when ingested. It complemented cold and humid foods such as meats.

Mustard is also an emetic; it causes vomiting. Kronos, the Titan of time in Greek mythology, had six children with his sister and wife Rhea: Demeter, Hades, Hera, Hestia, Poseidon and Zeus. Kronos' mother, Gaia, warned him that one of his children would overthrow him. Kronos became so angry about his childrens' power that he decided to eat them. He ate all but Zeus, because Rhea hid the baby, secretly swapping the young god for a rock instead. Once Zeus was grown up, he fed Kronos an emetic drink – a mixture of mustard, salt and honey – to make him vomit the contents of his stomach. Zeus, using mustard, saved his siblings.[4]

Mustard was an important part of the Renaissance banquets enjoyed by the privileged classes and was identified with refined taste. After the Industrial Revolution, evolving manufacturing techniques made mustard widely available and less mythical. However, its perceived effect on digestion remained valid.

The remedies of mustard were not limited to the stomach. The Greek physician Dioscorides, in the first century AD, wrote in *De re medica* that mustard could heal everything from swollen tonsils to epilepsy. Mustard was applied in a variety of forms: mustard plasters, mustard poultices and mustard baths. The most common medicinal use of mustard through the centuries was the mustard plaster or poultice, once recommended by the Greek physician Hippocrates for treating bronchitis and pneumonia. Hippocrates prescribed mustard plasters applied like a bandage to fix phlegm, rheumatism and arthritis. The Roman scholar Pliny the Elder even suggested a poultice of ground mustard and vinegar for snakebite and scorpion stings. Mustard paste was applied on the affected area and the skin was wrapped with cloth. This way the treatment would produce heat and draw the poison out of the skin, although sometimes it heated the skin too much and caused burns.

The seventh-century Byzantine Greek physician Paul of Aegina, who is considered the father of early medical writing, detailed the uses of mustard in his medical encyclopedia *Medical Compendium in Seven Books*. Among the many benefits of mustard he describes are warming the habit (health or constitution) and relieving dullness of hearing, poor digestion and evacuation of phlegm. He mentions the use of mustard plasters on the back and belly as a preventative measure against melancholy, paralysis and affections of the heart.[5] In Arabia, mustard was equally recognized for its medicinal properties. The tenth-century Arab physician Ibn al-Jazzar, who became famous for his writings on Islamic medicine, recommended mustard as a hot remedy for stimulation of sneezing, which was seen as beneficial to get rid of various kinds of matter that may cause illness.[6]

Mustard plasters have been prepared in France, in England and other parts of Europe since the Middle Ages. From there the remedy spread to the New World, where it remained popular until the beginning of the twentieth century. Mustard powder was also used by veterinarians as a poultice for horses and bulls. In 1866 a French pharmacist, Paul Jean Rigollot, invented commercial mustard papers. His invention was called *sinapism*, an adhesive plaster containing powdered black mustard to be applied to a patient's skin as a counter-irritant. It was shown at the Universal Exhibition in Paris in 1867. Paris hospitals, military hospitals and the British and the French navies used these papers to help people suffering with respiratory diseases. The papers came in a tin and were called 'Rigollot's Paper' after the inventor.

Rigollot mustard plasters are still sold today in France under the name *sinapisme* as a decongestant and relief against symptoms of colds, coughs and bronchitis. Adults are advised to use two to three sheets per day, applying a sheet wetted with cold or lukewarm water – up to 40 degrees Celsius

Mustard plasters in a tin box by Deane's.

Metal box by Rigollot containing mustard papers used for poultices, 19th century.

($104°$F) – on the chest, back or throat (never on the breasts), covering them with a dry towel until the skin becomes red and warm (about eight to twelve minutes).

Other commercial mustards plasters, such as from Deane Plaster Company and Seabury & Johnson (a company founded by Robert Wood Johnson before he founded Johnson & Johnson with his brothers), were made in the U.S. at the end of the nineteenth century. Later, Johnson & Johnson and Musterole sold plasters to relieve aches, pain and congestion

The Colman's polar bear, advertisement from the 1950s.

until a less pungent alternative without mustard, Vicks VapoRub, came on to the market.

Mustard was used in baths, ointments and mouthwashes to treat many illnesses. *Médecine Domestique*, published in 1802 in Paris, proposed a foot bath of mustard and horseradish, a mouthwash of *l'eau de vie* and mustard for the paralysis of the tongue, and mashed mustard seeds for toothache.[7] A foot bath of mustard powder in hot water was a favourite in the UK to treat a cold until relatively recently. The idea is that by stimulation of circulation in the feet, a mustard bath can relieve congestion of the head and lungs.

The use of mustard in Nepal, like in India, Pakistan and Bangladesh, is mostly as oil for cooking. However mustard oil was also used in medicine and in the religious ceremonies

Ox-powered mill grinding mustard seeds for oil, India.

of the Vedic people of northern India. In Nepal, it has been used in rituals to wash and thus purify the head and body. Nepalese people massage their hair and aches and pains in their bodies with mustard oil. The oil is prepared by pressing cooked mustard seeds, which removes any of the odour or pungency familiar to mustard sauce.

In the central Nepalese Tharu culture, women receive tattoos from the elders of the tribe as part of a social ritual. It is said that they use a mixture of mustard oil and cow dung, stabbing the blend through the skin using a thorn from the neem tree, both mustard oil and neem tree acting as an antiseptic. Tharu believe that when they die they cannot take anything with them but their tattoos. On the way to heaven, if one finds hardships one can sell the tattoos and therefore make the journey to heaven more comfortable. Tattooing children at an early age is also believed to protect them from illness and evil spirits.

Mustard as an Allergen

Mustard is an allergen as much as a medicine. It is one of the major allergens that must be declared in ingredient lists whenever they appear in pre-packed food sold in Canada and the EU, including the UK, but not in the U.S. The major allergy-inducing proteins in mustard are heat-resistant and are not greatly affected by food processing. Mustard allergy is very rare, although it is somewhat prevalent in France and Spain.

Another allergen that can be present in mustard is the sulphites. Most commercial mustards have potassium metabisulphite and sodium metabisulphite added to preserve colour and taste, thereby enhancing shelf life. When present, sulphites are marked as allergens on labels, even though most people are not allergic to sulphites. They are used in many other foods, such as dried fruits and wine.

Mustard for Muscles

Mustard is not just a medicine of the past. These days, runners grab packets of mustard when they are racing to relieve muscle cramps. Cramps are believed to be caused by dehydration or by the deficiency of acetylcholine, a chemical compound made up of acetic acid and choline. Mustard contains acetic acid, as in vinegar, but also sodium as an electrolyte, and often turmeric, which is known for its anti-inflammatory properties. For this, runners in the U.S. choose French's mustard or sometimes pickle juice.

However, recent scientific studies suggest that muscle cramps are a neurological rather than a physiological event. They evaluated food extracts such as peppers, ginger, mustard and cinnamon for their ability to resolve exercise-associated muscle cramps and found that consuming these food extracts does not seem to affect plasma electrolyte concentrations. Instead, it is thought that these food extracts can activate transient receptor potential channels, a group of ion channels located in the mouth, oesophagus and stomach that regulate the flow of ions – that is, charged particles like sodium and potassium – across cell membranes, that are capable of disrupting hyper-excited motor neurons. It is said that muscles cramp because of these hyper-excited neurons. Recent evidence suggests that oral ingestion of cinnamon, peppers or mustard may reduce the intensity and/or duration of muscle cramps, presumably by dampening neuron excitability.[8] No matter the mechanism, the good news is that these studies support the myth that mustard can prevent or reduce muscle cramps. After all, most of us spread and slather mustard without thinking of its many health benefits. Next, we will see the more common uses of mustard around the world as a spice, sauce, oil and plant to please our palates.

Yellow mustard on sausages.

5
Mustard on the Menu

The ancient Greeks ate whole mustard seeds with their meat. The Romans ate mustard greens much like spinach, and seasoned meat sauces with mustard seeds. During most of the Middle Ages, when spices were very expensive and out of reach for common people, mustard was the poor man's spice. Today mustard is still an essential ingredient in the kitchen and utilized in many dishes in various forms – oil, seeds, sauce, condiment and greens – to give them flavour or a pungent kick. Mustard is also used for its functional properties in other sauces.

Mustard seeds have a high proportion of oil (about 40 per cent) and protein (about 25 per cent). They are also rich in fibre and antioxidants. Some of the compounds, especially in yellow mustard, have unique properties that make it an important, functional food ingredient. One of the compounds is the seed coats, called mucilage. Mucilage has the ability to absorb and hold liquid, which is important in the manufacturing of hot dogs and other prepared meats. Hence, mustard not only boosts the flavour of a hot dog from the outside but gives it structure from the inside. Another valuable characteristic of yellow mustard is its emulsifying property. Emulsifiers allow the suspension of one liquid in another, such as oil in

Pickled mustard seeds.

water, which is important for salad dressings and mayonnaise. Vinaigrettes are traditional oil-in-water emulsions made with oil, vinegar, other flavourings and mustard. The emulsifying ingredient here is mustard. Specifically, the network of naturally occurring mucilage in mustard emulsifies the oil and water. In addition to mustard, a common ingredient in vinaigrettes is honey. While honey is not an emulsifier, its thick consistency helps to stabilize the mixture.

Some of the most common sauces, such as mayonnaise, vinaigrettes, marinades, hollandaise and, of course, honey mustard sauces, contain mustard. Mustard is a way to add vinegar and salt into a sauce. It gives sauces not only flavour but a binding property. However, Hervé This, the father of molecular gastronomy, warns us that a mayonnaise must not contain mustard or else it would be called a *rémoulade*.[1]

In fact, works such as *Néo-physiologie du goût par ordre alphabétique; ou, Dictionnaire général de la cuisine française ancienne et modern* (A New Physiology of Taste, in Alphabetical Order), published in 1839, gave mayonnaise recipes that do not contain mustard. Mustard was instead added to *rémoulade, sauce verte* and *sauce Robert*.[2] In his *Guide Culinaire*, the first edition of which dates from 1902, Auguste Escoffier wrote a recipe for mayonnaise without mustard and used mustard instead in other sauces, such as *sauce Raifort* with horseradish and *sauce moutarde a la crème* with cream.[3] Escoffier describes *rémoulade* as a sauce made of mayonnaise and mustard (and capers, gherkins, parsley, chervil, tarragon and 'half a spoonful of anchovy oil').

How is it, then, that adding mustard to mayonnaise has become known as a French technique? It was *Le Répertoire de la cuisine*, a professional reference book by Théodore Gringoire and Louis Saulnier published in 1914, that mentioned the use of mustard in mayonnaise, and from there on it spread into the kitchens of France and abroad as the French mayonnaise.[4]

Cooking does not change the flavour of mustard, but it does reduce its pungency. Therefore, mustard is added towards

Mustard oil and seeds.

the end of cooking. It is better to not add delicately flavoured mustards to hot dishes. Dijon and *à l'ancienne* are among the more suitable types for cooking.

Mustard can be added to many dishes, and the very basic form of it is popular in soups, such as mustard soup from the Netherlands and northern Belgium. It is in these inglorious comfort foods that we find examples of home cooking with mustard. It is also in wartime stories where some of the dishes with mustard originate – such as the potted cheese (leftover crumbs of cheese, mixed with mustard and margarine, baked in the oven and served with biscuits or toast) of Britain's National Kitchens during the First World War, or the doughnuts the people of Leningrad made from mustard during the Second World War.

Mustard oil is used for cooking in many states in India, especially in Bengal and Kashmir. Some dishes are always cooked or topped with mustard oil, such as steamed fish, vegetables and puffed rice. The use of mustard oil is definitely uncommon in Western cuisines. In Europe, the sale of

Black mustard seeds.

Mustard bread.

mustard oil is prohibited or controlled because of the irritating qualities of the isothiocyanates it contains. In the U.S., its sale is banned.

Black mustard seeds are part of some traditional spice mixes, such as the Japanese *shichimi togarashi* (along with chilli; *sansho*, related to Sichuan pepper; poppy seed; nori seaweed; sesame seeds; ginger; and dried orange or mandarin peel) or the south Indian and Bengali five-spice mixture *panch phoron* (with cumin, fennel, nigella and fenugreek).[5] *Panch phoron* is tempered and added at the start or finish of cooking. Tempering of spices, called *tadka*, is done by heating them in hot oil or ghee. This makes them more fragrant. Bengalis extensively use a freshly ground pungent mustard pickle called *kasundi*, made with ground mustard, mustard oil, lemon juice or sour green mangoes that are preserved in the sun, traditionally served with greens, bitter gourds and rice.[6]

Another use of the mustard plant is its leaves. Specifically, the leaves and stems of the *Brassica juncea* species of mustard plant, cultivated also for brown mustard seeds and mustard oil, are the source of mustard greens. The greens have more names than one can muster – depending on sub-varieties: leaf mustard, Korean red mustard, Japanese giant red mustard, garlic mustard, snow mustard, curled mustard, *mizuna* with dissected leaves, large-petiole mustard, horned mustard, head mustard, root mustard, multi-shoot mustard and knobby swollen stem mustard (*zha cai* in Chinese and *takana* in Japanese). In one form or another this plant appears in Asian, European, American and African cuisine. Asian mustard greens are often stir fried. In India, the leaves are chopped and cooked with butter or ghee into *saag* to be eaten with bread like *roti* or *naan*. In Korea, mustard greens are salted, spiced and fermented with anchovy sauce into *gat kimchi*. In Nepal, they are pressure cooked with meats or pickled into *achar*. In southwest China, the fist-sized stems of *zha cai* are salted, rubbed in red chilli and pickled.

As an ingredient, spice or sauce, in its leaves, seeds or oil, mustard is so versatile that it is possible to find it in nearly all kitchens around the world. It is this versatility and availability that makes it so familiar, yet so exciting.

Recipes

Historical Recipes

Mustard in a Minute, by Apicius (*c.* first century AD)
From William Kitchiner, *Apicius Redivivus; or, The Cook's Oracle*
(London, 1817)

Mix very gradually together, in a marble or wedgewood mortar, an ounce of flour of mustard, with three tablespoonsful of milk (cream is better), half a teaspoonful of salt, and the same of sugar. Obs. – Mustard made in this manner is not at all bitter, and may therefore be instantly brought to table.

Keeping Mustard, by Apicius

Dissolve three ounces of salt in a quart of boiling water, and pour it hot upon two ounces of scraped Horseradish; cover down the jar, and let it stand twenty-four hours: strain, and mix it by degrees with the best flour of mustard, beat well together for a long time till of the proper thickness: put into a wide mouthed bottle, and stopped closely it will keep good for months.

Mustard Cure for Common Cold,
in Cases of Persistent Headache due to Catarrh
or Abundance of Humour in the Head

By Pliny (fourth century AD). From Faith Wallis, ed., *Medieval Medicine: A Reader* (Toronto, 2010)

Macerate two ounces of mustard seeds in sweetened vinegar for a whole day; take 30 stems of stavesacre, and six ounces of hyssop heads, and crush them up all together; add six ounces of skimmed honey and grind it up with a sufficient quantity of sweetened vinegar. Gargle with this for three days under a clear sky and take moderately watered wine and sweet foods.

Mustard Greens

Byzantine, sixth century. From Anthimus, *De observatio ciborum*, trans. Shirley Howard Weber (Leiden, 1924)

Mustard greens are good, boiled in salt and oil. They should be eaten either cooked on the coals or with bacon, and vinegar to suit the taste should be put in while they are cooking.

Sinab (Mustard Sauce)

Al-Baghdadi, tenth century. From *Annals of the Caliphs' Kitchens. Ibn Sayar al-Warraq'a Tenth-century Baghdadi Cookbook*, trans. Nawal Nasrallah (Leiden, 2007)

Pick over and sift through mustard seeds to get rid of dust, twigs, rotten seeds, and other impurities that might be in it. Pound the seeds thoroughly. If this proves to be difficult, add to the seeds a piece of cotton. This will make pounding them much easier. Once you finish pounding, add to the seeds an equal amount of walnuts, and continue pounding. Then pour as much as you like of vinegar and strain the mixture in a fine sieve. You will get fine mustard that is whiter than sea foam itself (*zabad*). Take the foam only, and add to it a little salt and serve it, God willing. Make *sinab* sauce with the remaining mix by adding pounded *zabib* (raisins) and vinegar, or sugar and vinegar. It will be fabulous indeed.

Palace Chicken with Mustard

Andalusian, thirteenth century. From *An Anonymous Andalusian Cookbook of the Thirteenth Century*, trans. Charles Perry, available at http://daviddfriedman.com

Cut up the chicken and place in a pot with salt and onion pounded with cilantro, oil, coriander seed, pepper and caraway; put it on the fire until it boils, and when it has boiled gently, add cilantro juice, vinegar, and *murri*, and let the vinegar be more than the *murri*; when it has cooked, pound peeled almonds fine and stir with egg and some pepper, green and dried ground coriander and a spoon of prepared mustard; pour all this into the pan and add three cracked eggs and take it to the hearthstone to rest for a while, and serve, God willing.

Honey Mustard

German, fourteenth century. From *Ein Buch von Guter Speise* (Stuttgart, 1844)

Flavour caraway seeds and anise with pepper and with vinegar and with honey. And make it gold with saffron. And add thereto mustard. In this condiment you may make *sulze* (pickled or marinated) parsley, and small preserved fruit and vegetables, or beets, which(ever) you want.

Mustard Sops (*Soupe en moustarde*)

By Taillevent, fourteenth century. From Guillaume Tirel, *The Viandier of Taillevent*, ed. Terence Scully (Ottawa, 1988)

Take the oil in which you fried or poached your eggs without shells, with wine and water and chopped onions fried in oil, and boil everything in an iron pan: then take crusts of bread, toast them on the grill, cut them into square pieces and add them to boil with the other; then strain your bouillon, and drain your sops and drop them on a plate (*var.:bowl*); then put a little very thick mustard into your bouillon pan and boil everything and pour it on top of the sops.

Camelina Mustard Sauce
By Taillevent

While Magninus recommended camelina sauce for roast rabbit and small chickens, Taillevent suggests using it also for kid, lamb, mutton and venison. *Le Ménagier de Paris* recommends preparing camelina sauce with vinegar during the summer and wine during the winter. The original camelina recipe by Magninus does not call for mustard.

Take mustard, red wine, cinnamon powder and enough sugar, and let everything steep together. It should be thick like cinnamon. It is good for any roast.

Lumbard Mustard (Honey Wine Mustard Sauce)
From *The Forme of Cury*, fourteenth century

Take mustard seed and wash it and dry it in an oven. Grind it dry and sieve it. Clarify honey with wine and vinegar and stir it well together and make it thick enough; and when you would use it make it thin with wine.

Mustard Recipe
From *Le Ménagier de Paris*, fourteenth century. From Gina L. Greco and Christine M. Rose, trans., *The Good Wife's Guide (Le Ménagier de Paris), A Medieval Household Book* (Ithaca, NY, 2012)

If you want to make a stock of mustard to keep for a long time, do it at harvest time, with mild must. Some say that the must should be boiled.

If you want to make mustard hastily in a villa, grind some mustard seed in a mortar and mix in some vinegar, and pour through a straining cloth. If you want it to be ready immediately, put it in a pot in front of the fire.

Should you want to take your time and make excellent mustard, put the mustard seed to soak overnight in decent vinegar, then grind it well in a mill, and then little by little add vinegar. If you have some spices left over from making aspic, clarry, hippocras, or sauces, grind them up with it, and then let it steep. [Aspic is jellied meat, poultry or fish, hippocras is spiced and sweetened wine, and clarry is a version of hippocras, using white or red wine and honey.]

Columella's Mustard

Fifteenth century. From Columella, Lucius Junius Moderatus,
De re rustica, ed. A. Millar (London, 1745)

Cleanse and sift mustard-seed carefully; then wash it with cold water; and, when it has been well washed, let it lie two hours in water; afterwards take it out; and, having squeezed the water out of it with your hands, throw it into a new mortar, or into one that is made very clean, and bruise it small with pestle. When you have bruised it, draw the whole mash together to the middle of the mortar, and press it down with your flat open hand; and, after you have compressed it, scarify it; and, having placed a few live coals upon it, pour nitred water upon it, that it may free it from all its bitterness and paleness; then raise the mortar, so that all the moisture may be drained out of it; after this put white sharp vinegar to it, and mix it thoroughly with the pestle, and strain it. This liquor does exceeding well for pickling of turnips. But, if you would prepare mustard for the use of great entertainments, when you have squeezed all the noxious juice of it, add the freshest pine-apples you can find, and almonds to it; and bruise them carefully together, and pour in vinegar upon them. So the other things as I said above. When you come to use this mustard, it will not only be very fit for sawce, but very beautiful and pleasing to the eye; for it is of an exquisite whiteness, if it be made with care.

Mustard Sauce in Bits

By Platina, fifteenth century. From Mary Ella Milham, trans., *Platina, On Right Pleasure and Good Health: A Critical Edition and Translation of De Honesta Voluptate et Valetudine* (Tempe, AZ, 1998)

Mix mustard and well-pounded raisins, a little cinnamon and cloves, and make little balls or bits from this mixture. When they have dried on a board, carry them with you whenever you want. Where there is a need, soak in verjuice or vinegar or must. This differs little in nature from those above.

Red Mustard Sauce

By Platina

Grind in mortar or mill, either separately or all together, mustard, raisins, sandalwood, toasted bits of bread, and a little cinnamon. When it is ground, soak with verjuice or vinegar and a bit of must, and pass through a sieve into serving dishes. This heats less than the one above and stimulates thirst but does not nourish badly.

Mustard

From Martino of Como, *The Art of Cooking: The First Modern Cookery Book*, ed. Luigi Ballerini, trans. Jeremy Parzen (Berkeley, CA, 2005)

Take some charlock [wild mustard, *Sinapis arvensis*] and soak for two days, changing the water often so that it becomes whiter; and take some almonds that have been properly peeled and crushed. Once they have been well crushed, add them to the mustard and then crush together well. Then take some good verjuice or vinegar and crush some bread white in it; then thin and pass through a stamine. Make it as sweet or as strong as you wish.

Red or Violet Mustard
From Martino of Como, *The Art of Cooking*

Take the charlock and crush well; and take some raisins and crush them also, as well as you can. Take a bit of toasted bread and a little sandalwood extract and some cinnamon, and a little verjuice or vinegar, and sodden wine, and thin this mixture; and pass through a stamine.

Mustard that Can Be Carried in Pieces on Horseback
From Martino da Como, *The Art of Cooking*

Take the charlock and crush as above, and take some raisins that have been well crushed; add some cinnamon and a few cloves to these things. Then you can make little round balls the size of those that you shoot with a crossbow, or square pieces of whatever size you like; let them dry for a little while on a table, and once dried, you can take them from place to place, as you wish. When you want to use them, you can thin them with a little verjuice, or vinegar, or cooked must, that is, sodden wine.

Italian Mustard
From *Cuoco Napoletano*, sixteenth century, trans. Terence Scully,
The Neapolitan Recipe Collection, Cuoco Napoletano (Ann Arbor, MI, 2000)

Get the seed which is called *sinapo* and steep it for a day or two, changing the water often; get blanched almonds and grind them up and put them with the mustard seed grinding it all together; then get good must syrup to make it sweet, and for a tart taste use verjuice, and strain everything and make it thick. Add spices if you want it with spices.

Balled Mustard for Trips

From *Cuoco Napoletano*

Get mustard seed, when it has steeped a day, grind it up with a handful of raisins, cloves, cinnamon and a little pepper, and with this paste form balls, small or large as a walnut; then set to dry on a board; when dry, you can take them when you go riding; to distemper them, use verjuice or must or wine or vinegar.

Sweet Mostarda (*Mostarda amabile*)

By Bartolomeo Scappi, sixteenth century. From Luigi Ballerini and Massimo Ciavolella, eds, *The Opera of Bartolomeo Scappi (1570): L'arte et prudenza d'un maestro cuoco (The Art and Craft of a Master Cook)*, trans. Terence Scully (Toronto, 2008)

Get a pound of grape juice, another pound of quince cooked in sugared wine, four ounces of apples cooked in sugared wine, three ounces of orange peel, two ounces of candied lime peel and half an ounce of candied nutmegs; in a mortar grind up all of the confections along with the quince and apples. When that is done, strain it together with the grape juice, adding in three ounces of clean mustard seed, more or less, depending on how strong you want it to be. When it is strained, add in a little salt, finely ground sugar, half an ounce of ground cinnamon and a quarter-ounce of ground cloves. It is optional just how mild or strong you make it. If you do not want to grind up the confections, beat them small. If you do not have any grape juice you can do it without, getting more quince and apples cooked as above.

Sauce Robert (Brown Mustard Sauce)

From Marie Antonin Carême. *L'art de la cuisine française au dix-neuvième siècle* [*c.* 1833–44] (Paris, 1854)

Finely dice 3 large onions and cook them in clarified butter until lightly coloured. Drain. Mix in some consommé and 2 large spoonfuls of *espagnole* sauce [a mother sauce in French cuisine made by dark brown roux, veal stock, pieces of beef, vegetables and seasoning]. When the sauce is properly reduced, add a little granulated sugar, a little pepper, some vinegar, and a tablespoon of Dijon-style mustard.

Modern Recipes

Tuscan Style Mostarda (*Mostarda all'uso Toscano*)

From Pellegrino Artusi, *Science in the Kitchen and the Art of Eating Well* (*La scienza in cucina e l'arte di mangiar bene*), trans. Murtha Baca and Stephen Sartarelli (Toronto, 2003)

For this recipe you need 2 kilograms (about 4 lb) of sweet grapes, ⅓ red and ⅔ white grapes, or all white.

Press the grapes as if you were making wine, and after a day or two, when the dregs have come to the surface, drain off the must.

1 kg (about 2 lb) red or reinette apples
2 large pears
240 g (about 1 cup) of white wine or better Vin Santo
120 g (about 4.2 oz) of candied citron
40 g (about 1.4 oz) of white mustard powder

Peel the apples and the pears, slice them thinly, then put on the fire in the wine and, when they have absorbed it completely, pour in the must. Stir often and when the mixture has reached a firmer consistency than for fruit preserves, let it cool and add the powdered mustard, which you will have dissolved in advance in a little hot wine, and the candied fruit, diced in tiny pieces. Keep in small jars covered with a thin film of ground cinnamon. Mustard can also be used at the table to stimulate the appetite and facilitate digestion.

Makes 500 ml (2 cups)

Pickled Mustard Seeds

With permission from ChefSteps, www.chefsteps.com

Pickled mustard seeds are also called poor man's caviar. They are sweet and sour, rather than pungent. You can prepare a big batch and use them on anything from pork cheeks to pastrami sandwiches to foie gras parfait. Their tangy taste will brighten up any fatty dish and add textural intrigue with a subtle caviar-like pop in your mouth.

> 350 ml champagne vinegar
> 150 ml water
> 100 g sugar
> 11 g salt
> 200 g yellow mustard seed

Make the pickling liquid by mixing the vinegar, water, sugar and salt until dissolved. Reserve.

Place the mustard seeds in a pot. Add enough water to cover. Bring to a boil, whisking constantly. Strain.

Repeat eight more times to remove the bitter tannins: pour the seeds back in the pot, add fresh water, bring to the boil and strain.

Transfer the strained mustard seeds to a container, and cover with the pickling brine. Serve immediately or store in brine for several days to improve the flavour. Pickled mustard seeds will keep in the fridge for months.

Makes 400 g

Mustard Ice Cream

Adapted from www.seriouseats.com, accessed 6 April 2018

> 125 ml (½ cup) cream
> 60 ml (2 fl. oz) milk
> ¼ tsp turmeric
> ½ tsp vanilla extract

2 tbsp honey

pinch salt

3 egg yolks

2 tsp brown sugar

2 tsp Dijon Mustard

2 tsp wholegrain mustard

Place the cream, milk, turmeric, vanilla, honey and salt in a heavy saucepan and slowly bring to boil, stirring occasionally. Whisk together the egg yolks and brown sugar in a large bowl, until thick and light in colour. Slowly mix in the hot milk and cream mixture into the egg mixture and then return to pan. Slowly warm over a low heat, stirring continuously until thick. Sieve the mixture into a large bowl and leave to cool. Once the mixture has cooled, stir in the mustards and place in the fridge. Put the mixture in an ice cream maker for 30 to 45 minutes. Transfer the mixture to a plastic container and place in the freezer for about 5 hours, or until frozen.

Mustard Bread (*Senf Brot*)
Recipe with permission from Karen Anderson of the blog
https://brotandbread.org

For the pre-ferment
140 g (1 cup) bread flour
84 g (3 fl. oz) water
¼ tsp instant yeast
¼ tsp salt

For the soaker
104 g (½ cup) wheat meal, coarse
70 g (⅓ cup) rye meal
130 g (4.4 fl. oz) water
¾ tsp salt

For the final dough
all preferment
all soaker
556 g (2 cups) bread flour
15 g instant yeast
3¼ tsp salt
408 g (2 cups) water
66 g (¼ cup) mustard
122 g (4 oz) middle-aged Gouda (eighteen months old), coarsely grated or cut in chunks
mustard for brushing
sunflower or pumpkin seed for topping

Day One: In the morning, mix pre-ferment and soaker. Cover bowls, and leave them at room temperature. In the evening, mix all final dough ingredients at low speed (or by hand) for 1–2 minutes, until all flour is hydrated. Let rest for 5 minutes, then knead at medium-low speed (or by hand) for 6 minutes, adjusting with a little more water or flour, if necessary (dough should be somewhat sticky, clearing only sides of bowl, but stick to bottom). Transfer dough to a lightly oiled work surface. With oiled hands, stretch and pat it into a square, first fold top and bottom in thirds, like a business letter, then do the same from both sides. Gather dough into a ball, place seam side down into a lightly oiled bowl, cover, and let it rest for 10 minutes. Repeat this stretching and folding 3 times, with 10 minute intervals. After last fold, place dough in lightly oiled container with lid and refrigerate overnight.

Day Two: Remove dough from fridge 2 hours before using. Preheat oven to 240°C (464°F), including baking stone and steam pan. Place seeds for topping on a plate. Shape dough into 2 boules, brush them with mustard, and then roll them in sunflower or pumpkin seeds. Place breads, seam side down, on parchment lined baking sheet, and let them proof, until they have grown 1½ times their original size. Bake for 15 minutes, steaming with 1 cup of boiling water. Remove steam pan, and rotate breads 180 degrees. Reduce temperature to 210°C (410°F) and continue baking for another 25 minutes, or until breads are a deep reddish brown, sound hollow when thumped at the bottom, and register at least 93°C (199°F). Let breads cool on a wire rack.

Groninger Mustard Soup

1 clove garlic, finely chopped
1 medium-sized onion, finely chopped
50 g (¼ cup) butter
100 ml (4 fl. oz) cream or crème fraîche
1 litre (4.2 cups) vegetable stock
150 g (1 cup) bacon cubes
1 leek
3 tbsp coarse grain mustard
50 g (½ cup) cornflour (cornstarch)

Melt the butter in a soup pan and sauté the onion and garlic for a few minutes. Add the flour and slowly pour in the stock to create a smooth emulsion. Allow to cook for a minute or two and then add the cream. Bring this to boil. Cut the leek in half and then in thin slices. Add the leek and the mustard and stir. Let it boil for about four more minutes on low heat. Add a pinch of salt and pepper to your taste. Fry the bacon in a frying pan until crisp. Serve the soup garnished with crispy bacon bits.
Serves 4

Punjabi Mustard Greens (*Sarson ka saag*)
Adapted from Meera Sodha, *Fresh India: 130 Quick, Easy and Delicious Vegetarian Recipes for Every Day* (London, 2016)

250 g (1 cup) double cream
1 kg (2.2 lb) mustard leaves, cut into strips
1 tbsp vegetable oil for frying
2 large onions, finely chopped
1 tbsp ginger, peeled

6 garlic cloves, crushed
1 tbsp cumin seeds
½ tsp turmeric powder
1 tsp chilli powder
½ tsp salt

Add mustard greens and enough water to a saucepan, cover and bring to the boil. Reduce to a simmer for 15 minutes, or until they are tender. Strain using a strainer and drain well. Blend in a mixer with 4 tablespoons of water to form a thick paste. Heat the oil in pan and add the cumin seeds. When the seeds crackle, add the garlic and ginger and sauté on a medium flame for 30 seconds. Add the onions and sauté for another 2 minutes or until the onions are translucent.

Add mustard greens, turmeric powder, chilli powder, and salt to the pan, mix well, and cook for 2–3 minutes at low heat. Serve it hot with corn roti.

Serves 4

References

1 The Meaning of Mustard

1 Donna Demaio, 'Quantas 787 Dreamliner Takes Off Fuelled by Mustard Seed Biofuel on Los Angeles–Melbourne Flight', *Traveller*, www.traveller.com.au, accessed 29 January 2019.
2 At https://atlas.media.mit.edu, accessed 28 January 2019.
3 Kelli C. Rudolph, ed., *Taste and the Ancient Senses (The Senses in Antiquity)* (London, 2017), p. 186.
4 Ruth A. Johnston, *All Things Medieval: An Encyclopedia of the Medieval World* (Santa Barbara, CA, 2011), vol. I, p. 255.
5 Terence Scully, 'Tempering Medieval Food', in *Food in the Middle Ages: A Book of Essays*, ed. Melitta Weiss Adamson (New York, 1995), pp. 3–23.
6 Magninus, *Opusculum de saporibus*, available at www.staff.uni-giessen.de, accessed 27 February 2018.
7 Ken Albala, *Eating Right in the Renaissance* (Berkeley, CA, 2002), p. 253.
8 Harold McGee, *On Food and Cooking: The Science and Lore of the Kitchen* (New York, 2004), p. 394.

2 The Mustard Manual

1 Kelli C. Rudolph, ed., *Taste and the Ancient Senses (The Senses in Antiquity*) (London, 2017), p. 133.

2 Comité des travaux historiques et scientifiques, *Collection de documents inédits sur l'histoire de France publiés par ordre du roi et par les soins du Ministre de l'instruction publique; rapports au roi et pièces* (Paris, 1835), available at https://archive.org, accessed 6 November 2017.

3 Alexandre Dumas, 'Étude sur la Moutarde, par Alexandre Dumas', in *Le Grand Dictionnaire de Cuisine, 'Annexe'* (Paris, 1873) *Annexe*, pp. 3–11.

4 Ruth Cowen, *Relish: The Extraordinary Life of Alexis Soyer, Victorian Celebrity Chef*, Kindle edn (London, 2010).

5 Alexis Soyer, *Memoirs of Alexis Soyer: With Unpublished Receipts and Odds and Ends of Gastronomy* [1859], ed. F. Volant and J. R.Warren (New York, 2013), p. 252.

6 Vic Van de Reijt, *Willem Elsschot: De mosterdverzen* (Amsterdam, 2013).

7 Sir Hugh Plat, *Delightes for Ladies to Adorn Their Persons, Tables, Closets, and Distillatories, With Beauties, Banquets, Perfumes, and Waters* (London, 1644), available at the Library of Congress, www.loc.gov, accessed 9 April 2018.

8 Arthur Hill Hassall, *Food and Its Adulterations: Comprising the Reports of the Analytical Sanitary Commission of The Lancet* (London, 1855), p. 124.

9 Thomas Fuller, *The History of the Worthies of England, in Three Volumes* (London, 1662), vol. 1, available at https://archive. org, accessed 15 April 15 2018.

10 See www.tewkesburymustard.co.uk, accessed 22 September 2017.

11 Michael Bateman, *A Delicious Way to Earn a Living* (London, 2008).

12 Colma's of Norwich, *Information Guide No. 3,* Unilever Archives and Records, Port Sunlight (date unknown).

13 Advertisement 'The Mustard Club Topical Budget' (Publicity films: Norwich, Norfolk, 1926), East Anglian

Film Archive of the University of East Anglia, www.eafa.org.uk, accessed 2 March 2018.

14 Darra Goldstein, *The Oxford Companion to Sugar and Sweets* (New York, 2015), p. 463.

15 *Liber de Coquina*, Part 1: *Tractatus*, recipe 12, trans. Thomas Gloning, vol. x (2001), available at www.staff.uni-giessen.de, accessed 28 February 2018.

16 *Liber de Coquina*, Part 2: *Liber de Coquina,* recipes 13, 14, trans. Thomas Gloning, vol. x (2002), available at www.staff.uni-giessen.de, accessed 28 February 2018.

17 Martino da Como, *The Art of Cooking: The First Modern Cookery Book*, trans. Jeremy Parzen (Berkeley, CA, 2005), p. 135.

18 Terence Scully, ed., *The Neapolitan Recipe Collection (Cuoco Napoletano)* (Ann Arbor, MI, 2000), p. 180.

19 Cristoforo di Messisbugo, *Libro novo* (Venice, 1557), p. 85.

20 Luigi Ballerini and Massimo Ciavolella, eds, *The Opera of Bartolomeo Scappi (1570): L'arte et prudenza d'un maestro cuoco (The Art and Craft of a Master Cook),* trans. Terence Scully (Toronto, 2008).

21 Michel De Montaigne, *Viaggio in Italia*, trans. Ettore Camesasca, digital edn (Milan, 2013).

22 Ippolito Cavalcanti, *Cucina Teorico-pratica*, 2nd edn (Naples, 1839), pp. 253–4, available at https://archive.org, accessed 1 March 2018.

23 Pellegrino Artusi, *Science in the Kitchen and the Art of Eating Well (La scienza in cucina e l'arte di mangiar bene)*, trans. Murtha Baca and Stephen Sartarelli (Toronto, 2003).

24 Pauline B. Lewicka, 'Description of mustard (*sifat khardal*)', in *Food and Foodways of Medieval Clairenes: Aspects of Life in an Islamic Metropolis of the Eastern Mediterranean* (Leiden, 2011), pp. 277–8.

25 Ibid., p. 345.

26 The Canon of Medicine (*Al-Qanun fi al-tibb*) of Avicenna, reprinted from the 1930 edn (New York, 1973), available at https://archive.org, accessed 10 April 2018.

27 Ogier Ghislain de Busbecq, *Türk Mektuplari*, trans. Derin Türkömer (Istanbul, 2005), available at https://kupdf.net, accessed 13 September 2018.

28 Alden T. Vaughan, *New England Frontier: Puritans and Indians, 1620–1675*, 3rd edn (Norman, OK, 1995), p. 6.

29 Mentioned in three Lewis and Clark journal entries (Joseph Whitehouse 7 April 1805, Lewis Meriwether 5 June 1806 and William Clark 5 June 1806). Journals of the Lewis and Clark Expedition. Available at www.lewisandclarkjournals. com, accessed 27 October 2017.

30 Sylvester Graham, *Lectures on the Science of Human Life*, vol. II (Boston, MA, 1839), pp. 595–8.

31 Andrew F. Smith, 'Condiments', in *The Oxford Encyclopedia of Food and Drink in America*, 2nd edn, ed. Andrew F. Smith (Oxford, 2012), p. 459.

32 Ellen G. White, *The Ministry of Healing* (Guildford, 2011), p. 209.

33 Andrew F. Smith, ed., *Savoring Gotham: A Food Lover's Companion to New York City* (New York, 2015).

34 Donovan A. Shilling, *Made in Rochester* (Rochester, 2015), pp. 174–6.

35 Barry Levenson, personal conversation, 10 January 2018.

3 Mustard in Language and Literature

1 John Ayto, ed., *Oxford Dictionary of English Idioms*, 3rd edn (Oxford, 2009), p. 193.

2 Ibid., p. 84.

3 Eric Partridge, *The Routledge Dictionary of Historical Slang*, ed. Jacqueline Simpson (ebook, London, 2006).

4 Harold V. Cordry, *The Multicultural Dictionary of Proverbs* (Jefferson, NC, 2005), pp. 160, 162.

5 Kelli C. Rudolph, ed., *Taste and the Ancient Senses (The Senses in Antiquity)* (London, 2017), p. 41.

6 Robert Beer, *The Handbook of Tibetan Buddhist Symbols* (London, 2003), p. 25.

7 Eugene Watson Burligame, trans., Charles Rockwell Lanman, ed., *Buddhist Legends*, Part 1, *Translated from the Original Text of the Dhammapada Commentary* (Delhi, 2005), p. 107.

8 Gerard Schroeder, *Genesis and the Big Bang: The Discovery of Harmony between Modern Science and the Bible* (New York, 1990), p. 65.

9 Herbert Lockyer, *All the Parables of the Bible* (Grand Rapids, MI, 1963), pp. 186–7.

10 Pliny, *Natural History*, vol. V: *Libri XVII–XIX*, trans. H. Rackam (Cambridge, MA, 1950), pp. 529, 531, available at https://archive.org, accessed 11 January 2018.

11 Robert A. Kittle, *Franciscan Frontiersmen: How Three Adventurers Charted the West* (Norman, OK, 2017), p. 44. See Thomas C. Patterson, *From Acorns to Warehouses: Historical Political Economy of Southern California's Inland Empire* (Oxford, 2016).

12 Hadith 165 in *The Book of Faith (Kitab Al-Iman)*, trans. Abdul Hamid Siddiqui, at www.theonlyquran.com, accessed 12 January 2018.

13 François Rabelais, *Gargantua and Pantagruel*, vol. 1, p. 116, at www.readhowyouwant.com, accessed 2 November 2016.

4 Mustard in Myths and Medicine

1 William Crooke, *An Introduction to the Popular Religion and Folklore of Northern India* (New Delhi, 1994).

2 Samuel Noah Kramer, *The Sumerians: Their History, Culture and Character* (Chicago, IL, 1963), pp. 96–7.

3 Hippocrates, *Hippocrates,* vol. IV, trans. W.H.S. Jones (Cambridge, MA, 1967), p. 331.

4 Julia Wolfe Loomis, *Mythology* (New York, 1965), p. 12.

5 Paulus Francis Adams, *The Medical Works of Paulus Aegineta, the Greek Physician* (London, 1834), available at https://archive.org, accessed 19 March 2018.

6 Gerrit Bos, *Ibn Al-Jazzar on Forgetfulness and its Treatments* (London, 1995), p. 25.

7 Jean-Denis Duplanil, *Médecine domestique. Ou, Traité complet des moyens de se conserver en santé, et de guérir les maladies par le régime et les remèdes simples: ouvrage mis à la portée de tout le monde* (Paris, 1802), pp. 74, 79, 326. Available at https://archive.org, accessed 8 November 2017.

8 Jun Qiu and Jie Kang, 'Exercise Associated Muscle Cramps – A Current Perspective', *Scientific Pages of Sports Medicine*, 1/1 (2017), pp. 3–14.

5 Mustard on the Menu

1 Hervé This, *Kitchen Mysteries: Revealing the Science of Cooking*, trans. Jody Gladding (New York, 2010), p. 42.

2 Anonymous, *Néo-physiologie du gout par ordre alphabétique, ou dictionnaire général de la cuisine française ancienne et modern,* 2nd edn (Paris, 1853), available at http://gallica.bnf.fr, accessed 7 November 2017.

3 Auguste Escoffier, *Le Guide Culinaire: aide-mémoire de cuisine pratique avec la collaboration de MM. Philéas Gilbert and Émile Fétu,* 3rd edn (Paris, 1912), pp. 52, 209, available at http://gallica.bnf.fr, accessed 7 November 2017.

4 T. H. Gringoire and L. Saulnier, *Le Répertoire de la cuisine,* 3rd edn (London, 1923), p. 19, available at http://gallica.bnf.fr, accessed 7 November 2017.

5 Harold McGee, *On Food and Cooking: The Science and Lore of the Kitchen* (New York, 2004), p. 398.

6 Chitrita Banerji, *Bengali Cooking: Seasons and Festivals* (London, 1997), pp. 29, 60.

Select Bibliography

Albala, Ken, *Eating Right in the Renaissance* (Berkeley, CA, 2002)

Anonymous, *Néo-physiologie du gout par ordre alphabétique, ou dictionnaire général de la cuisine française ancienne et modern,* 2nd edn (Paris, 1853)

Ballerini, Luigi, and Massimo Ciavolella, eds, *The Opera of Bartolomeo Scappi (1570): L'arte et prudenza d'un maestro cuoco (The Art and Craft of a Master Cook),* trans. Terence Scully (Toronto, 2008)

Banerji, Chitrita, *Bengali Cooking: Seasons and Festivals* (London, 1997)

Carême, Marie Antonin, *L'art de la cuisine française au dix-neuvième siècle* [1833–44] (Paris, 1854), pp. 103–4

Cavalcanti, Ippolito, *Cucina Teorico-pratica,* 2nd edn (Naples, 1839)

Child, Julia, Louisette Bertholle and Simone Beck, *Mastering the Art of French Cooking* (New York, 1961), vol. 1

Columella, Lucius Junius Moderatus, *De re rustica,* ed. A. Millar (London, 1745)

Dumas, Alexandre, 'Étude sur la Moutarde, par Alexandre Dumas', in *Le Grand Dictionnaire de Cuisine, 'Annexe'* (Paris, 1873)

Escoffier, Auguste, *Le Guide Culinaire: aide-mémoire de cuisine pratique, avec la collaboration de MM. Philéas Gilbert and Émile Fétu,* 3rd edn (Paris, 1912)

Gringoire, T. H., and L. Saulnier, *Le Répertoire de la cuisine,* 3rd edn (London, 1923)

Kitchiner, William, *Apicius Redivivus; or, The Cook's Oracle* (London, 1817)

Lewicka, Pauline B., 'Description of Mustard (*ṣifat khardal*)', in *Food and Foodways of Medieval Clairenes: Aspects of Life in an Islamic Metropolis of the Eastern Mediterranean* (Leiden, 2011)

McGee, Harold, *On Food and Cooking: The Science and Lore of the Kitchen* (New York, 2004)

Martino of Como, *The Art of Cooking: The First Modern Cookery Book,* trans. Jeremy Parzen (Berkeley, CA, 2005)

Messibugo, Cristoforo di, *Libro novo* (Venice, 1557)

Milham, Mary Ella, trans., *Platina, On Right Pleasure and Good Health: A Critical Edition and Translation of De Honesta Voluptate et Valetudine* (Tempe, AZ, 1998)

Pegge, Samuel, *The Forme of Cury: A Roll of Ancient English Cookery Compiled, about AD 1390* (London, 2008)

Pliny, *Natural History,* vol. v: *Libri XVII–XIX,* trans. H. Rackam (Cambridge, MA, 1950)

Rudolph, Kelli C., ed., *Taste and the Ancient Senses (The Senses in Antiquity)* (London, 2017)

Scully, Terence, 'Tempering Medieval Food', in *Food in The Middle Ages: A Book of Essays,* ed. Melitta Weiss Adamson (New York, 1995), pp. 3–23

Smith, Andrew F., ed., *Savoring Gotham: A Food Lover's Companion to New York City* (New York, 2015)

This, Hervé, *Kitchen Mysteries: Revealing the Science of Cooking,* trans. Jody Gladding (New York, 2010)

Tirel, Guillaume, *The Viandier of Taillevent,* ed. Terence Scully (Ottawa, 1988).

Wallis, Faith, ed., *Medieval Medicine: A Reader* (Toronto, 2010)

Websites and Associations

English Mustard Growers
www.englishmustardgrowers.co.uk

Mustard Club of Cincinnati
www.mustardclub.org

The National Mustard Museum
www.mustardmuseum.com

The Saskatchewan Mustard Development Commission
www.saskmustard.com

Brands

Colman's
www.colmans.co.uk

French's
www.frenchs.com

Maille
https://fr.maille.com

La Moutarderie Fallot
www.fallot.com

Moutarde de Meaux Pommery
www.moutarde-de-meaux.com

Tewkesbury Mustard
www.tewkesburymustard.co.uk

Acknowledgements

This book is a tribute to the half-year I spent working in the mustard factory of Amora and Maille in Dijon in 2008. My stay in Dijon instilled in me a love for the yellow condiment (and Burgundy wine), and steered my career in a more culinary direction.

Information about mustard is scattered around the world like its seeds: it is everywhere and plentiful. Many people helped me access a seed of the mustard history. I am grateful to Ruth Loughrey and Lucy Myatt from Unilever Archives, Andréa Luccisano from Unilever Marketing, Marc Désarménien from Edmond Fallot, Natalie Veranneman from Vve Tierenteyn-Verlent bvba, and Bernard Desrumaux from Mostaardfabriek Ferdinand Tierenteyn bvba. Berry Levenson, the founder of the National Mustard Museum, kindly shared his vast knowledge about the world of mustard. Christine Peres from Musée de la vie Bourguignonne helped with historical images. Professor Ken Albala helped with historical references and Latin translations. Marie Sophie Zwart, Matteo Europeo, Nicolas Ladrange, Lynn Archer and Rahul Shinde contributed with valuable fact checking. Series editor Andrew Smith and publisher Michael Leaman made this a better book with their invaluable comments and suggestions.

Finally, I am grateful for my husband Luca for his endless support and enthusiasm to taste a mountain of mustard with me. During this time our son Adriano entered our lives, bringing with him much love and a final insight on mustard – that healthy baby poop is bright mustard yellow!

Photo Acknowledgements

The author and the publishers wish to express their thanks to the below sources of illustrative material and /or permission to reproduce it.

Karin Anderson of hanseata.blogspot.com: p. 107; ©Amora Collection: p. 33; Courtesy of Zosia Brown: p. 40; Namiko Chen of www.justonecookbook.com: p. 65; Demet Güzey: p. 32; Develey Company: p. 44; Courtesy of Edmund Fallot Mustard Makers: p. 37; Istockphoto: p. 6 (undefined undefined); Luise Händlmaier GmbH: p. 45; Hudson-Fulton Celebration Commission Records: p. 69; Courtesy of Barry Levenson of the Mustard Museum: pp. 75, 76, 77, 93; Los Angeles County Museum of Art (LACMA): p. 90; © Maille Collection: p. 35; The Metropolitan Museum of Art, New York: pp. 16, 17; McCormick & Company, Inc: p. 73; Musée de la Vie Bourguignonne Perrin de Puycousin, Dijon: pp. 13, 28, 30, 32, 34, 87, 96 (Photos F. Perrodin), 81; National Gallery of Art, Washington, DC: p. 79; Paris Museum Collection: p. 25; Saskatchewan Mustard Development Commission: pp. 11, 23, 102 (Renée Kohlman), 104 (Renée Kohlman); © The Board of Trustees of the Science Museum: p. 92; © SPERLARI: p. 59; Courtesy of Tierenteyn-Verlent: p. 41; Unilever Archives: pp. 49, 52, 53, 54, 56, 97; Courtesy of Van Gogh Museum, Amsterdam (Vincent van Gogh Foundation): p. 43; Wellcome Collection: p. 84; Wikimedia Commons: pp. 38 (Fonquebure CC BY-SA 3.0), 67 (Czar), 98

Index